Praise for
21 Things You Need to Know About Indigenous Self-Government

"In this book, Bob Joseph once again captures the facts and importance of Indigenous Peoples rights to self-government. He outlines why it is imperative that all Canadians understand that when Indigenous Peoples reclaim their rightful place in decision-making and self-determination, all Canadians will benefit from a more just and inclusive Canada."

Nancy C. Southern,
chair and chief executive officer, ATCO

"Bob Joseph's new book is indispensable for all Canadians, Indigenous and non-Indigenous alike, entering into a conversation about alternatives to the *Indian Act*."

Bruce McIvor, *author of* Indigenous Rights in One Minute: What You Need to Know to Talk Reconciliation

"Bob Joseph has done it again. Shifting focus from the oppressive federal *Indian Act*, he provides an effective analysis of the tools that will support Canada's commitment to reconciliation—self-government. Joseph has a remarkable ability to distill historic and complex legal issues into an impactful narrative that will resonate with the reader. This is a must-read for anyone who wants to better understand where Indigenous communities are planning to go."

Clint Davis,
CEO, Cedar Leaf Capital Inc.

21

A CONVERSATION ABOUT DISMANTLING THE INDIAN ACT

21 THINGS

THINGS

YOU NEED TO KNOW
ABOUT INDIGENOUS
SELF-GOVERNMENT

BOB JOSEPH

INDIGENOUS RELATIONS PRESS

Copyright © 2025 by Bob Joseph

All rights reserved. No part of this book may be reproduced, stored in a retrieval system or transmitted, in any form or by any means, without the prior written consent of the publisher or a licence from The Canadian Copyright Licensing Agency (Access Copyright). For a copyright licence, visit accesscopyright.ca or call toll free to 1-800-893-5777.

21 Things™, the RESPECT™ model, and Working Effectively with Indigenous Peoples® are registered trademarks of Indigenous Corporate Training Inc.

Cataloguing in publication information is available from Library and Archives Canada.
ISBN 978-1-77458-627-3 (paperback)
ISBN 978-1-77458-628-0 (ebook)

Indigenous Relations Press
ictinc.ca
Saanichton, BC

Page Two
pagetwo.com

Page Two™ is a trademark owned by Page Two Strategies Inc., and is used under license by authorized licensees

Cover design by Peter Cocking
Interior design by Peter Cocking and Fiona Lee
Printed and bound in Canada by Friesens
Distributed in Canada by Raincoast Books
Distributed in the US and internationally by Macmillan

25 26 27 28 29   5 4 3 2 1

*To the dignified who suffered the indignities
of assimilation and to those who honour their memory
by pursuing truth and reconciliation for the long term,
to build a brighter future for all our kids.*

CONSERVATIVE MP HENRY HERBERT STEVENS:

Q: Supposing the aboriginal title is not recognized? Suppose recognition is refused, what position do you take then?

PETER KELLY, HAIDA NATION:

A: Then the position that we would have to take would be this: that we are simply dependent people. Then we would have to accept from you, just as an act of grace, whatever you saw fit to give us. Now that is putting it in plain language. The Indians have no voice in the affairs of this country. They have not a solitary way of bringing anything before the Parliament of this country, except as we have done last year by petition, and it is a mighty hard thing. If we press for that, we are called agitators, simply agitators, trouble makers, when we try to get what we consider to be our rights. It is a mighty hard thing, and as I have said, it has taken us between forty and fifty years to get to where we are to-day. And, perhaps, if we are turned down now, if this Committee see fit to turn down what we are pressing for, it might be another century before a new generation will rise up and begin to press this claim.

During the Special Joint Committee on
Claims of Allied Indian Tribes of BC, April 4, 1927

For the record—

"Everything about us without us" is the Indian Act.

"Everything about us by us" is self-government and that's what we're going to talk about.

Also by Bob Joseph

21 Things You May Not Know About the Indian Act

Indigenous Relations
(Bob Joseph with Cynthia F. Joseph)

Working Effectively with Indigenous Peoples®
(Bob Joseph and Cynthia F. Joseph)

Contents

Introduction *1*

Part 1 · Where We've Been, Where We Are, Where We're Going

From Royal Proclamation
to Forced Assimilation *7*

We Are Simply Dependent *17*

What Is Self-Government? *21*

Part 2 · 21 Things About Indigenous Self-Government

1 The United Nations Declaration
on the Rights of Indigenous Peoples
Sets the Standard *31*

2 Treaties and Self-Government
Differ but Relate *35*

3 Self-Government Aligns With Sovereignty *41*

4 The Trustee-Wardship
Relationship Dissolves *43*

5	Reserve Realities Change	45
6	Laws of General Application Apply	49
7	Traditional Leadership Is Tied to Community	53
8	Nations Have the Right to Choose Their People	61
9	Nations Determine Their Financial Checks and Balances	67
10	The Fiduciary Duty Diminishes	71
11	Tax Is Included	79
12	Indigenous Rights Include Language Rights	83
13	Socio-Economic Issues Can Be Remedied	91
14	The Infrastructure Gap Closes	99
15	Self-Reliance and Economic Reconciliation Can Begin with Small Actions	105
16	Free, Prior, and Informed Consent Must Be Obtained	117
17	Territories Can Overlap	125

18	Self-Administration Is Not Self-Government.....	*127*
19	Supporting Self-Government Is an Economic and Moral Opportunity......................................	*129*
20	Local Governments Can Support Self-Government..................................	*135*
21	Self-Government Is Achievable..........................	*139*

APPENDIX 1: Join the Conversation!.................. *143*

APPENDIX 2: Questions from Indigenous Youth.. *147*

APPENDIX 3: Additional Reading...................... *149*

APPENDIX 4: United Nations Declaration on the Rights of Indigenous Peoples................... *151*

Acknowledgements *169*

Notes *171*

Index *187*

Introduction

~~~~~~~

THANK YOU for reading this book and joining the conversation on Indigenous self-government. First and foremost, this is not a technical book on how to dismantle the *Indian Act*. This book aims to gain support from readers like you for understanding why the Act needs to be dismantled. I will take you on a journey from the early days when Indigenous Peoples were self-governing, self-determining, and self-reliant, to the dark days under the *Indian Act*, and to what the future can look like as Indigenous Nations return to self-government, self-determination, and self-reliance.

The *Indian Act* has constrained and controlled the lives of Status Indians for generations. Reconciliation will be hampered with the *Indian Act* intact. This legislation, consolidated in 1876 and amended many times since, is the albatross around the neck of reconciliation. I hope, by the end of this book, you will understand why we can't just get rid of it and why we need to dismantle it while still honouring Canada's fiduciary duty to Status Indians.

Before we go any further, I want to clarify the different usages of "self-determination." In the terminology of the United Nations Declaration on the Rights of Indigenous Peoples, self-determination includes governance. My view on self-determination comes from my Kwakwaka'wakw heritage, in which giving names to our people makes them citizens of our nation. So, throughout this book, "self-determination" means the right to choose who your people are.

The hundreds of thousands of you who read *21 Things You May Not Know About the Indian Act*[1] and participated in online and in-person presentations often had questions like "What's next?" "Can we get rid of it?" "What would it look like?" and "Will it work?" I was also curious about what kinds of questions our Indigenous Corporate Training Inc. newsletter subscribers had about self-government, so the team sent them a survey. We received over 150 questions on self-government. Now more than ever, these questions are timely, especially given that 2026 marks 150 years since the consolidated *Indian Act, 1876*, and I have been hearing from many in the Indigenous community that dismantling the *Indian Act* is especially relevant.

So can it be done? I'm going to show you how it's achievable and that the 21 Things provided here aim to answer that question and others. The process has already begun, and there's a solid foundation to build upon. There are many examples of self-government and constitutions in place, and some of them have been around for a long time.

I'm grateful you have taken the time to read this book because we need this conversation to generate more understanding, more support, and more political will for dismantling the *Indian Act* and moving towards even more self-government for Indigenous Peoples.

As a country, we have charted a path towards Indigenous self-government, and when we follow it completely, we will be able to hold our heads high because we will have addressed this historic injustice, and created more economic certainty and opportunity that will set up our country for success and make life better for all Canadians now and in the future.

Read this book, share your knowledge, and join the conversation. Let's put our foot on the gas pedal and change our country in a way that I believe will benefit our country for the next seven generations of all our children.

Gilakas'la,
K'AXWSUMALA'GALIS*
BOB JOSEPH

*(whale who emerges itself from the water and presents itself to the world)

PART

>>>>>>>>>>>>>|<<<<<<<<<<<<<

WHERE WE'VE BEEN, WHERE WE ARE, WHERE WE'RE GOING

>>>>>>>>>>>>>|<<<<<<<<<<<<<

From Royal Proclamation to Forced Assimilation

TO UNDERSTAND where we've been, we need to step back a few hundred years to when King George III issued the Royal Proclamation of 1763. This Proclamation set the stage for modern constitutional recognition and protection of Indigenous Rights (broadly thought of as the practices, traditions, or customs integral to an Indigenous society's distinctive culture that were practised prior to European contact) in Canada. The Proclamation spells out how the relationship between Europeans and Indigenous Peoples began, including the very important statement that Indigenous Peoples were recognized as nations of people.

In the Royal Proclamation, King George III makes a number of significant statements but for our purposes here, the most significant is the paragraph that says: "And whereas it is just and reasonable, and essential to Our Interest and the Security of Our Colonies, that the several Nations or Tribes of Indians, with whom We are connected, and who live under Our Protection, should not be *molested* or *disturbed* in the Possession of such Parts of

Our Dominions and Territories as, not having been ceded to, or purchased by Us, are *reserved* to them, or any of them, as their *Hunting Grounds*."[1] (emphasis added)

1763	1867	1982
Royal Proclamation	**Confederation**	*Constitution Act*
Nation to Nation	Wards of the Crown	Nation to Nation
Recognition	Assimilation	Recognition and Affirmation
Treaties	*Indian Act*	Aboriginal and Treaty Rights

The Proclamation was King George III's way of securing military and economic alliances from and building and maintaining loyalties with Indigenous Peoples. It encouraged widespread support from Indigenous Peoples as essential trading and military partners, for England; and the Proclamation reduced loyalties to the French, Spanish, and Russians. It was essential in helping King George III prevail over these competing colonizing and trading interests.

But, at Confederation in 1867, Canada abandoned the principles of the Royal Proclamation. There was a fundamental shift, from the view of nations or tribes with whom the colonizers were connected who were not to be molested or disturbed—with their fishing and hunting rights and treaties intact—to the view that Indigenous Peoples were savages, incapable of governing themselves or raising their own children; their only salvation was assimilation into European society. How did we go from the Proclamation to this other place of forced assimilation and cultural genocide, as described by The Right Honourable Beverley McLachlin, PC, former Chief Justice of Canada, on the eve of the Truth and Reconciliation Commission of Canada's final national event: "In the buzz-word of the day, *assimilation*; in the language of the 21st century, *cultural genocide*"?[2] (emphasis added)

Change began when Canada became a country, with the issuance of the *British North America Act*, or what is now known as the *Constitution Act, 1867*.[3] Indigenous Peoples were valuable economic alliances to King George III because of their role in the robust fur trade. But when the fur trade disappeared, their economic value diminished, just as it did earlier when their military support was no longer as valuable.

Around the time of Confederation, Indigenous communities were also being hit hard by disease and depopulation, in part because of their interactions with Europeans and in part because of their being removed from their traditional lifestyles and diets and forced to live within the constraints of reserves.

There are differing opinions about the number and source of the earliest arrival of the smallpox virus and ensuing epidemics. Some historians say there was an epidemic in the north in the 1770s, introduced by sea,[4] and another in the south in 1781–82, introduced by land.[5] What everyone agrees upon, however, is that the Indigenous population had no immunity to the virus. The close confines of winter homes provided ideal conditions for the virus to devastate entire communities. People died at such a rate that it became impossible to bury the dead according to traditions, which led to mass burials.[6] Eventually, those too became unmanageable, and the dead were left where they died.[7] Community members who fled to avoid the sickness took it with them, thereby spreading the infection.

It is estimated that about 30,000 First Nations people lived on the coastline of British Columbia before a smallpox epidemic struck in 1862; post-epidemic, that number dropped to 15,000.[8] On the West Coast alone, one smallpox epidemic killed up to 80 to 90 per cent of some local Indigenous populations, including Semá:th and Stó:lo First Nations,[9] and another epidemic followed a few years later, further decimating their numbers.[10] But sadly, the devastation was not restricted to the coast. Through trade and travel, the smallpox virus spread to almost every First Nations community in Canada.

Suffice it to say, at the time of Confederation, the stage was set for Canada to believe that Indigenous Peoples were a dying race of people who were not fitting in militarily or economically and that it should help facilitate their transition, or assimilation, into the new country.

When the *Indian Act* was consolidated in 1876, it was based on a paternalistic position:

> Our Indian legislation generally rests on the principle that the aborigines are to be kept in a condition of tutelage and *treated as wards or children of the State*. [...] True interests of the aborigines of the State alike require that every effort should be made to aid the Red man in lifting himself out of his condition of tutelage

and dependence, and that it is clearly our wisdom and our duty, through education and every other means, to *prepare him for a higher civilization* by encouraging him to assume the privileges and responsibilities of full citizenship.[11] [emphasis added]

It was assumed that the assimilation process would be speedy, that Indigenous Peoples would embrace the opportunity to exchange their traditions and culture for those of the European settlers, and it would work out. But that is not what happened.

After Confederation and into the late 1800s and 1900s, *Indian Act* assimilation amendments became more aggressive—women were targeted, children were taken, traditional leadership was replaced, and cultural activities were outlawed. These increasingly restrictive and aggressive amendments were driven by zealots who built their careers by pushing harsh policies. One example is the establishment of Indian residential schools to assimilate children under strict and forbidding policies before they could reach adulthood. The tragedy of children dying at the residential schools should not have occurred, and despite reports from medical officers about the conditions of the schools and the high rate of death among the children, it continued unabated. The reports were quashed.[12]

So, we ended up in this really dark place with the *Indian Act*, of which, until more recently, most Canadians were largely unaware. In training offered by my organization, Indigenous Corporate Training Inc., which we deliver all across the country, we do an exercise during which we ask people to jot down on a flip chart the history of Indigenous Peoples as they know it, to create a timeline.

More often than not, there's about an 80-year gap in the common knowledge of history, from the late 1800s to the early 1960s. That timeline gap coincides with the period when the full legislative power of the Canadian state was pushing forward, full steam ahead, with forced cultural assimilation. Most Canadians were unaware of this policy of cultural assimilation because the state intentionally hid the shameful way it was treating Indigenous Peoples.

Canada, by the late 1960s, realized that the policy of assimilation was not working and that Indigenous Peoples were not going to assimilate. Ironically, the very policies geared to assimilation were the exact restrictions that kept First Nations separate from mainstream society. If you want to assimilate people, don't put them on separate lands and make them live under separate laws, which the *Indian Act* did. A change of policy direction was taking place.

In 1969, the Government of Canada released the *Statement of the Government of Canada on Indian Policy*, otherwise known as the "White Paper,"[13] which called for the removal of the *Indian Act*, the transfer of reserve lands—over which the federal government had exclusive jurisdiction under the *Constitution Act, 1867*—to individuals, and the removal of the federal government's fiduciary duty. Its creators regarded the White Paper as the final instrument in the long-standing policy of Indian assimilation. Remember, if assimilation was successful, there would be no need to negotiate new treaties or self-government agreements, nor to honour historic treaties. It was an important moment because, for the first time in over 100 years, the federal government mentioned the future of the country without the *Indian Act*.

However, Chiefs from all across the country rejected the White Paper. They were concerned that it implied that the federal government was going to cut them loose at one of the worst periods in their history. After decades of enforced assimilation, enforced dependency, and intergenerational trauma, First Nations were lacking resources and without the capacity to be self-reliant. They were not going to let the federal government off the hook of the existing trustee-wardship relationship until both parties could agree upon a way to move forward. The rejection of the White Paper highlighted a policy challenge for the federal government and the Chiefs. What now? What do we do about the *Indian Act*? These questions would eventually lead to self-government negotiations.

With no small pressure from Indigenous groups, in 1982, Canada decided to patriate the constitution and include section 35, which recognizes and affirms existing Indigenous and treaty rights. This watershed moment marked the end of forced cultural assimilation, although the *Indian Act* continued to exist with the restrictions far outweighing the benefits—an imbalance that continues to this day. Section 35 states:

Section 35 of the *Constitution Act, 1982*

35. (1) The existing aboriginal and treaty rights of the aboriginal peoples of Canada are hereby recognized and affirmed.

Definition of "aboriginal peoples of Canada"
(2) In this Act, "aboriginal peoples of Canada" includes the Indian, Inuit and Métis peoples of Canada.

Land claims agreements
(3) For greater certainty, in subsection (1) "treaty rights" includes rights that now exist by way of land claims agreements or may be so acquired.

Aboriginal and treaty rights are guaranteed equally to both sexes
(4) Notwithstanding any other provision of this Act, the aboriginal and treaty rights referred to in subsection (1) are guaranteed equally to male and female persons.[14]

The country is still wrestling with the issue of the federal government's exclusive jurisdiction, via the *Constitution Act, 1867*, over "Indians, and Lands reserved for the Indians."[15] So, now the question is, How do we end this trustee-wardship relationship?

The repatriated constitution opened a door for the Supreme Court of Canada to weigh in on issues related to Indigenous Rights and Indigenous Title (the rights of Indigenous Peoples to the occupation, use, and enjoyment of their land and its resources). The underlying belief was that once treaty and Indigenous Rights were recognized as "constitutional rights," they would be constitutionally and legally protected from political interpretations. In reality, the burden fell upon Indigenous Peoples to define, largely through litigation, the nature and quality of those rights. Currently, we see a combination of legal challenges to and negotiated settlements about historical grievances and current issues. In my opinion, we need to do more negotiated settlements and fewer litigated settlements. Litigation doesn't necessarily allow for dynamic and customized agreements. It focuses on specific issues and sets precedents that may not be best in all circumstances. I believe that lawyers and the law are important, but lawyers and the law should codify the agreements Indigenous Peoples make for themselves and not lead the process of reconciliation.

We Are Simply Dependent

~~~~~~~~~~~~~~~~

JUST BEFORE the introduction, I shared a question asked by Conservative MP Henry Herbert Stevens and an answer provided by Peter Kelly of Haida Nation in 1927, during the Special Joint Committee on Claims of Allied Indian Tribes of BC. Peter Kelly's response to Stevens's question about the position, if recognition of Aboriginal Title was refused, was "then the position that we would have to take would be this: that we are simply dependent people."[1]

Given the historical and ongoing trauma of living under the *Indian Act*, why aren't more, if not all, Indigenous communities, with the support of their citizens, striving to move away from the *Indian Act* and towards self-government? Hesitation may stem from concerns about transparency and accountability in Nations' leadership elected under *Indian Act* rules. If a community's leadership lacks transparency and accountability and it moves to being completely self-governed, how could it build transparency and accountability after the fact?

People are reluctant to take the chance. They want transparency and accountability to be in place before they can begin to consider self-government. Fear of the unknown and ingrained dependency are also factors. There's that old expression "better the devil you know than the devil you don't."

In many communities, families and friends of the Elected Chief and Council may have concerns about how things are being run on the reserve but may be hesitant to speak up out of concern for offending the chief. This situation is one reason why the *Indian Act*-imposed Elected Chief and Council system can be problematic.

Dependency is the outcome of the intergenerational trauma of the *Indian Act*. The playbook for trauma goes all the way back to Confederation, specifically section 91(24) of the *British North America Act*, now known as the *Constitution Act, 1867*.[2]

Section 91(24) is what gave the Crown the jurisdiction over "Indians, and Lands reserved for the Indians" that I mentioned earlier. This all-important section is the legal basis for the trustee-wardship relationship. The government set itself up as the trustee for the bands, and members of the bands became wards of the Crown. In this type of relationship, there is an imbalance of power, with one party (the Crown) having more power than the other (Indians). In a perfect world, trustees act in the best interests of their wards, but that is not how this particular relationship works.

A more recent perspective on this is presented in the book *Dances with Dependency: Out of Poverty Through Self-Reliance* by Calvin Helin, an Indigenous author.[3] I love the title because it nails the harmful side effects of being a ward of the Crown. You become completely dependent.

You are not self-reliant nor self-determining, and you're certainly not self-governing if you are living under the *Indian Act*.

Calvin Helin's thoughts on dancing with dependency are poignant. Before the *Indian Act*, Indigenous Peoples were independent, but over time, they became very dependent. Not because they wanted to but because the *Indian Act* structured their dependency. *Indian Act* legislation has had a negative effect emotionally, spiritually, and psychologically on generations of Indigenous Peoples and specifically Status Indians, as defined by the Act.

So, you may ask, why don't people just leave the reserve and this dependent relationship? When asked that question, I like to share an analogy I heard. It is a story about the old days of travelling circuses. The circus would come to town and set up its tents and put up pens for its animals. A young elephant calf, too young to be in an act, would be tied by a foot to a stake in the ground. For weeks and weeks, it would try as hard as it could to break free from that stake, but it just couldn't, so it eventually would give up and accept the situation. All the while, the elephant calf would grow bigger and bigger. It could easily pull the stake out of the ground and walk away, but it learned a long time ago that it couldn't break free of what was holding it back.

The emotional, psychological, and spiritual devastation of the *Indian Act* framed the idea that breaking free is impossible, unless you give up your status or identity, so people just stopped trying and accepted the situation for what it was, and that frame of mind continued for generations.

The Restrictions Outweigh the Benefits

The *Indian Act* is trying to get rid of Status Indians. It has done so historically through assimilation, enfranchisement, an ever-narrowing eligibility criteria for status, and the inability to pass along status to the next generation. Currently, the *Indian Act* cuts off the right to registration as a Status Indian when an individual has one parent and one grandparent (two consecutive generations) who are not registered as Status Indians. This is called the two-generation rule. It is absolute and does not account for the community the individual is connected to. This is not how Indigenous groups determine membership. Over time, the two-generation rule under the *Indian Act* will eliminate Status Indians from the official government register.

For a lot of people, gaining status is considered a worthy goal because of the so-called benefits. I don't agree that there are benefits. We should think of the so called benefits as restrictions instead. But because the *Indian Act* creates a cycle of dependency, it can be hard to see the "benefits" as restrictions. We need to break free from this cycle and start to think about a world beyond the *Indian Act*.

So, how do we break free from the *Indian Act*? By dismantling it through self-government agreements that include self-governance, self-determination, and self-reliance.

What Is Self-Government?

~~~~~~~~~~~~~~~~

Long before European contact, Indigenous Peoples had their own established political systems and institutions—they were self-governing, self-reliant, self-determining, and decided who was in their nations or who their people were. Many Indigenous communities have been trying to regain the right to govern themselves and preserve their cultural identities ever since the *Constitution Act, 1867*. This Act gave the federal government the authority to make laws about "Indians, and Lands reserved for the Indians"—in other words, the Act applied Euro-Canadian ideals, policies, and laws to Indigenous societies. In 1887, Nisga'a and Tsimshian Chiefs journeyed to Victoria, BC, to request treaties and self-government. They were denied, but they continued to lobby the government and tried to seek remedy in the courts. It would not be until the year 2000, 113 years later, that the Nisga'a Final Agreement (2000)[1] went into force. While the Nisga'a Final Agreement is a treaty, it is also a vehicle of self-government. I admire the patience and persistence of Indigenous Peoples.

Self-government agreements return decision-making powers to Indigenous governments so they can, once again, make their own choices about how to deliver programs and services to their citizens and communities. These decision-making powers can include protecting their citizenship, culture, and language; educating their students; managing their lands; and developing new business partnerships to generate jobs and additional benefits for their citizens. Canada tried to take these rights away with the *Indian Act*, so it makes sense that Indigenous Nations are trying to regain them.

Indigenous Peoples today consider the return to self-government to be foundational to nation-building. These agreements are critical to communities that want to contribute to and participate in the decisions that affect their lives. "Nothing about us without us."

The struggle for self-government has been ongoing for a long time. Prior to 1973, the Government of Canada refused to even entertain the concept of Indigenous self-government. It was the Supreme Court of Canada's ruling in *Calder et al. v. Attorney General of British Columbia*[2] that caused a shift in policy (see the sidebar "Aboriginal Title in the *Calder* Case"). Even then, however, the federal government sought to narrow the interpretation and restrict the scope of Indigenous self-government to a legislatively based approach: that is, to ensure that any form of self-government that might result from negotiations would come into existence as a legislative grant by the Parliament of Canada and, therefore, would operate "at the pleasure of Parliament" and be subject to parliamentary amendment.

ABORIGINAL TITLE IN THE *CALDER* CASE

For many years, the Government of Canada denied the concept of Aboriginal[3] Title ("the inherent Aboriginal right to land or a territory").[4] That policy mountain moved in 1973, shortly after the release of the Supreme Court of Canada's landmark decision in *Calder et al. v. Attorney-General of British Columbia*.

In the *Calder* case, the Nisga'a Tribal Council asked the courts to support its claim that Aboriginal Title had never been extinguished in the Nass Valley, near Prince Rupert, BC.

Although the Supreme Court of Canada ultimately dismissed the Nisga'a case on a technicality, the case is historic because, for the first time, Canada's highest court ruled that Aboriginal Title was rooted in the "long-time occupation, possession and use" of Traditional Territories. As such, Aboriginal Title existed at the time of original contact with Europeans and at the time of the formal assertion of British sovereignty in 1846.

Shortly after the *Calder* decision, the Canadian government agreed to begin negotiating a treaty with the Nisga'a to define their rights to land and resources and relationships with other governments.

Indigenous Peoples often refer to self-government as an "inherent" right, pre-existing in Indigenous occupation and governance of the land before European settlement. Some Indigenous Peoples balk at the concept of the Canadian and provincial governments granting them self-government because they believe the Creator gave them the responsibilities of self-government and that right has never been surrendered—it was taken by government legislation. In this light, Indigenous self-governance does not have to be recognized by federal or provincial governments because the right simply exists. Self-government agreements frequently begin with "the effective date of the self-government agreement is..." Some interpret the use of the phrase "effective date" as the government of Canada granting self-government, while Indigenous Peoples consider that date a recognition of self-government.

In August 1995, the Government of Canada formally recognized the inherent right of self-government for Indigenous Peoples by releasing "The Government of Canada's Approach to Implementation of the Inherent Right and the Negotiation of Aboriginal Self-Government," which provides, in part, the following:

> The Government of Canada recognizes the inherent right of self-government as an existing Aboriginal right under section 35 of the *Constitution Act, 1982*. It recognizes, as well, that the inherent right may find expression in treaties, and in the context of the Crown's relationship with treaty First Nations. Recognition of the inherent right is based on the view that the Aboriginal peoples of Canada have the right to govern themselves in relation to matters that are

internal to their communities, integral to their unique cultures, identities, traditions, languages and institutions, and with respect to their special relationship to their land and their resources.[5]

Attaining a self-government agreement is not easily done. There is no "one-size-fits-all" template. There was an attempt in the first session of the 41st Parliament (June 2011 to September 2013) to introduce the *First Nations Self-Government Recognition Act* (Bill S-212),[6] but it died on the order paper with the ending of that session of Parliament.

At the time of writing, there are 25 self-government agreements across Canada involving 43 Indigenous communities. And there are approximately 50 self-government negotiation tables at various stages of the negotiation process, and in many cases being negotiated in conjunction with modern treaties.[7]

Here are three examples of self-government agreements, all of which meet my litmus test of success—that is, you rarely hear about them in the news.

The James Bay and Northern Quebec Agreement (1975)

The James Bay and Northern Quebec Agreement[8] was the first modern Indigenous land claim agreement and treaty in Canada, and it is protected by the Canadian Constitution. Cree treaty rights set out in the Agreement cannot be changed or abolished without Cree consent.

"The James Bay and Northern Quebec Agreement contains 31 chapters covering such subjects as eligibility, land regime, local and regional government, health and education, justice and police, environmental and social protection, hunting, fishing and trapping rights, community and economic development, an income security program for Cree trappers and a special forestry regime."[9] Since its signing, the Agreement has been amended by 24 Complementary Agreements to adapt it to the changing needs of the Cree Nation.

The Nisga'a Final Agreement (2000)

The Nisga'a Final Agreement was signed in 1998 and came into force in May 2000, conveying fee simple title (freehold ownership) to 2,000 square kilometres of the Nass Valley; creating separate jurisdictions within that territory for the Nisga'a Nation and the Nisga'a villages; and giving the Nisga'a Nation defined powers to co-manage hunting, fishing, and trapping rights in a much larger area (called the "Nass Wildlife Area"). The Nisga'a Final Agreement is subject to the *Canadian Charter of Rights and Freedoms*. In addition, the Nisga'a Nation has no jurisdiction to make criminal laws.

The Nisga'a Final Agreement has become an inspiration to Indigenous Peoples around the world. Joseph Gosnell, key Nisga'a negotiator and Hereditary Chief of the Eagle Clan, writes:

> News of the Nisga'a Final Agreement has traveled far beyond the Nass Valley—across British Columbia, Canada, and around the world. Governments and aboriginal peoples are all watching the implementation of our treaty with keen interest. They are also

seeking the advice of Nisga'a negotiators and government members. Aboriginal people from North, South, and Central America, Taiwan, Australia, and Scandinavia have all traveled to the Nass Valley to see Nisga'a government in action and to learn first-hand from the Nisga'a experience. The treaty is an inspiration for our people and other First Nations. We take great pride in this accomplishment.[10]

As of May 11, 2000, the *Indian Act* ceased to apply to the Nisga'a people.

The Westbank First Nation Self-Government Agreement (2005)

With the signing of the 2005 Westbank First Nation Self-Government Agreement,[11] the Westbank First Nation became a true nation with the right to govern its own affairs, and the responsibility to make decisions affecting the well-being of the community while being held accountable to its electorate.

The Westbank First Nation Government provides services for over 10,000 residents living on Westbank First Nation lands, 10,000 of whom are non-band members with residential leases on Westbank lands.[12] The Westbank First Nation Government is one of the most progressive First Nation governments in Canada with a comprehensive set of laws that cover items such as land use, zoning, and local government services that mirror municipal services for its residents, including law enforcement, snow removal, recreation, utilities, and public works. In addition, the Agreement covers matrimonial and property rights, language and culture, resource management and the environment, land management, and taxes.

The Westbank First Nation Self-Government Agreement also contains a provision confirming the application of the *Canadian Human Rights Act*[13] to Westbank First Nation lands and members; the First Nation takes all necessary measures to ensure compliance of its laws and actions with Canada's international legal obligations.

To Each Their Own

While self-government is not a quick fix for the deeply rooted social, health, and economic issues that plague Indigenous communities, it is a step towards empowering communities to break free from the constraints of the *Indian Act* and rebuild and heal from the intergenerational effects of residential schools.

Though self-government agreements may contain common elements, there can be no cookie-cutter approach to them. Future and forthcoming agreements will not all be exactly the same because each will address the priorities of the nation to reshape its social and economic well-being. Common elements could be education, health care, child protection, social services, housing, police services, and property rights.

Self-government is a relatively unfamiliar concept for many Canadians so I'm sure there are lots of questions about what exactly it looks like and how self-governing nations will impact the fabric of Canada. Let's now look at part 2, "21 Things About Indigenous Self-Government," that can inform the vision for a better country.

PART

>>>>>>>>>>>>>|<<<<<<<<<<<<<

21 THINGS ABOUT INDIGENOUS SELF-GOVERNMENT

>>>>>>>>>>>>>|<<<<<<<<<<<<<

{ 1 }

The United Nations Declaration on the Rights of Indigenous Peoples Sets the Standard

> The United Nations Declaration on the Rights of Indigenous Peoples is the *framework for reconciliation* at all levels and across all sectors of society.[1] [emphasis added]

THE UNITED NATIONS Declaration on the Rights of Indigenous Peoples (the "UN Declaration") is an international human rights instrument that sets the minimum standard for the treatment of Indigenous Peoples and states that the rights contained within it "constitute the minimum standards for the survival, dignity and well-being of the indigenous peoples of the world."[2] The UN Declaration includes 24 preambular paragraphs and 46 articles. It is a significant milestone in the march to protect and promote Indigenous Rights. You can read the UN Declaration in its entirety in Appendix 4.

The United Nations General Assembly, after more than two decades of dedicated negotiations, adopted the UN Declaration in 2007. This significant event was not without its challenges. Although 144 states voted in its favour, marking a significant step forward, not all states were on board. There were four objector states: Canada, Australia, New Zealand, and the United States.

Of most significant concern for the Government of Canada were provisions dealing with lands, territories, and resources; Free, Prior, and Informed Consent when used as a veto (note that the word "veto" is not used in the UN Declaration); self-government without recognition of the importance of negotiations; intellectual property; military issues; and the need to achieve an appropriate balance between the rights and obligations of Indigenous Peoples, member states, and third parties.

In 2010, in a significant shift, the Government of Canada, led by the Conservatives, endorsed the UN Declaration. However, it stated that the UN Declaration was an aspirational document, not legally binding, and not reflective of customary law.[3] This stance changed in 2016 when the Liberal government, then in power, announced its full support of the UN Declaration without qualification.[4] It pledged to adopt and implement the UN Declaration in accordance with the Canadian Constitution. This commitment was further solidified in 2021 when the *United Nations Declaration on the Rights of Indigenous Peoples Act* received royal assent and immediately came into force.[5] With this, Canada committed to ensuring that all federal laws reflect the standards set out in the United Nations Declaration on the Rights of Indigenous Peoples. This includes, by right, the *Indian Act*.

The UN Declaration promotes and protects the rights and freedoms, and recognizes the collective rights, of Indigenous Peoples worldwide. Yet, when you read the articles, it is easy to feel as though it was written solely for Indigenous Peoples in Canada.

The table below shows that the central themes of the UN Declaration address the central themes of the *Indian Act*. And this is not happenstance. Many Indigenous leaders in Canada spent much time working on the development of the UN Declaration.[6]

Indian Act themes	UN Declaration themes
Displaced traditional governance systems	The right to self-determination
Enforced assimilation	The right to be recognized as distinct peoples
Did not consult on projects in Indigenous Peoples Traditional Territories	The right to Free, Prior, and Informed Consent
Segregated people onto reserves	The right to be free from discrimination

The United Nations Declaration on the Rights of Indigenous Peoples is the framework for reconciliation. It is also the foundation for self-government, self-determination, and self-reliance.

{ 2 }

Treaties and Self-Government Differ but Relate

~~~~~~~~~~~~~~~~~

THERE CAN BE confusion about treaties and self-government agreements and the relationship between them. Explanations can get pretty dry, so I will keep them brief. I am including a short history lesson to set the stage, so be warned.

Treaties

Modern treaties (post-1973), sometimes known as comprehensive land claims, are nation-to-nation relationships between Indigenous Peoples, the federal government, and provincial or territorial governments. They primarily concern land. These treaties are different from historic treaties because they were negotiated and entered into after the Supreme Court of Canada recognized Aboriginal rights for the first time in the *Calder* case.

When looking at historic treaties (1701 to 1973), we must remember the era and the intent of the parties involved. The Indigenous leaders who "marked" the historic treaties—they did not sign them, as signing a document was an alien concept for oral societies that depended on people honouring their verbal commitments—knew the world for future generations of their people was changing. They negotiated in good faith for the survival of their people.

The Chiefs or traditional leaders negotiated for what they anticipated would be needed as they transitioned from their formerly expansive, self-determining, self-governing, and self-reliant world to subsistence- and dependence-living on small reserves—in other words, to becoming wards of the state. The treaty articles they negotiated included education, economic assistance, health care, livestock, agricultural tools, and agricultural training. As Menno Boldt notes in his book, *Surviving as Indians: The Challenge of Self-Government*:

> The chiefs who marked the treaties profoundly believed themselves to be entrusted by the Creator with the protection of their tribal cultures—the Creator's blueprint for their survival and well-being. When they participated in the treaty-making process they did so from the conviction that they were honouring this sacred trust. In their minds, the treaty was an instrument for fulfilling this sacred obligation to the Creator, to their ancestors, and to generations yet to come. Another implicit understanding of the chiefs who marked the treaties was that they were autonomous peoples, and that the treaties affirmed the continuity of their autonomy. They marked the treaties in the spirit of coexistence, mutual obligation, sharing, and

benefit, and as an agreement between themselves and the newcomers not to interfere in each other's way of life. They assumed the treaties would enshrine this *intent* and *spirit* as a permanent and living legacy. Thus, as a frame of reference for justice, the treaties provide a paradigm of high idealism.[1] [emphasis added]

The other signatory, the Crown, had a different intent. Under John A. Macdonald, Canada's first prime minister, the intent was to remove Indigenous Peoples from their land, gain access to natural resources, open up the country for settlers, and construct a railway from Upper Canada to the Pacific Ocean. The Crown representatives, working from their European concept of land as a transferable commodity, viewed treaties as real estate agreements. Boldt continues:

[The Crown] entered the treaty-making process with the spirit and intent of achieving an atmosphere of peace and stability that would facilitate settlement, real-estate speculation, and commerce with the objective of making huge fortunes in the new land. Consistent with this view, the Crown's representatives were negotiating lucrative "real-estate deals" with Indians for huge tracts of land which it then opened up for settlement and commercial exploitation. In short, each side entered the treaty-making process with a different "spirit and intent."[2]

Modern treaties, or comprehensive land claims, are negotiated in a dramatically different setting. Negotiators speak a common language. Indigenous negotiators can hire lawyers (which was prohibited under the *Indian Act* from 1927 to 1951)[3] and have constitutionally and legally acknowledged Indigenous Title to land they have occupied since time immemorial.

Self-Government

Self-government is an inherent right for Indigenous Peoples in Canada, constitutionally confirmed in section 35 of the *Constitution Act, 1982*.[4] Self-government agreements create new government-to-government relationships with Canada, including governing structures, a constitution, elections, and accountability mechanisms. It returns decision-making powers to an Indigenous nation's government, which makes its own choices about delivering programs and services to its communities. This can include decisions about better protecting its culture and language, educating its students, managing its own lands, developing revenue-generating structures, and creating new business partnerships that generate jobs and other benefits for its citizens.[5]

The route to self-government can take different paths. Historic and modern treaties can exist without self-government. Treaty 8 is an example. Treaty 8 people, which include First Nations in northeastern British Columbia, northern Alberta, northwestern Saskatchewan, and part of the Northwest Territories,[6] are still governed by institutions created by the federal government—Elected Chiefs and Councillors—and in that sense, they're not self-governing, but they have a treaty.

A self-government agreement can be in place while a treaty is negotiated. Treaties can take decades to conclude. For example, the shíshálh Nation entered into a self-government agreement[7] while it waited to conclude its treaty negotiations. Once its treaty negotiations were concluded, the Nation simply attached the self-government agreement to the treaty as a chapter. The process to self-government occurred in stages.

Self-government also can exist outside of treaties as it did in the case of the Westbank First Nation Self-Government Agreement. Or self-government agreements can be seen inside and part of a treaty, as with the Nisga'a Nation, which successfully dismantled its ties with the *Indian Act* and replaced it with its own form of government.[8]

{ 3 }

Self-Government Aligns With Sovereignty

SELF-GOVERNING NATIONS continue to be a part of the fabric of Canadian society. All the agreements that have been negotiated to date between Canada and Indigenous Peoples are within the Canadian Confederation. There has been no attempt through the negotiated self-government agreements to remove self-governing nations from a sovereign Canada. Self-government is about Indigenous Nations having more control over their lives and livelihoods, not about separating from Canada.

I like this quote from *The Unjust Society* by Harold Cardinal, author and Cree leader, because it presents a perspective on sovereignty that is often missed:

> The vast majority of our people are committed to the concept of Canadian unity and to the concept of participation in that unity. The Indians of Canada surely have as great a commitment to Canada, if not a greater

one, than even the most patriotic-sounding political leaders. More truly than it can be said of anyone else, it is upon this land that our heritage, our past and our identity originates. Our commitment to Canada exists because of our belief that we have a responsibility to do all we can to ensure that our country is a nation with which we can proudly identify.[1]

Harold Cardinal uses the words "vast majority," indicating that there may be a small number of communities who would be interested in living in a nation-state—to be a country within a country—but there currently is no mechanism for them to pursue it. Canada, as a nation, has neither a mandate nor a political will to negotiate that kind of sovereignty.

It's not a separatist movement.

One last thought related to this topic: Sovereignty is a complex concept in Canada. During the lead-up to the 1995 Quebec sovereignty referendum, the Cree First Nations in Quebec were very active in those conversations. One of the things they said was that if Quebec were to separate, the Cree would then separate from Quebec and take their ancestral lands with them.

It was an interesting procedural manoeuvre—would the Cree take their lands out of Quebec and join Canada? Because the referendum failed, we don't know what that might have looked like.

{ **4** }

The Trustee-Wardship Relationship Dissolves

I AM OFTEN ASKED, "Why are people still treated like wards of the federal government?" This question cuts to the reason why we want to see Indigenous Nations return to self-government.

When section 91(24) of the *Constitution Act, 1867* gave the Crown jurisdiction over "Indians, and Lands reserved for the Indians," it set up an imbalance of power, with the government as the trustee for the bands.[1] Members of the bands became wards of the Crown.

The attitude of the day was to "make things better for Indians"—to help them assimilate into the culture of and become like the colonizers. Indians were considered wards until they assimilated. The fathers of Confederation did not have the foresight, insight, or interest to consider that Indians might not be willing to give up their culture, identity, lands, and resources.

Ironically, the *Indian Act*, which was supposed to make Indians a part of the cultural mainstream of Canada, created the opposite situation. It separated Indigenous Peoples and kept them living on separate lands and under separate laws. This is the great paradox of the *Indian Act*.

So, the short answer about why many First Nations communities are still functionally wards of the Crown is that the relationship was created through a constitutional and legal system, and we have not yet found a way to "uncreate" it. Eliminating section 91(24) and the trustee-wardship relationship means eliminating the *Indian Act*, which can be achieved only through amending the Canadian Constitution. As evidenced by the rejection of the 1992 Charlottetown Accord, which was to address Quebec's concerns and to recognize Indigenous self-government, amending the Constitution is a very difficult process.

We can eliminate the trustee-wardship relationship and bypass the process of amending the Constitution by negotiating self-government agreements.

{ 5 }

Reserve Realities Change

A RESERVE IS a tract of federally held Crown land set aside under the *Indian Act* for the exclusive use of an Indian band. Earliest examples of reserves date back to 1637 and to attempts by French missionaries to encourage Indigenous Peoples to settle in one spot and embrace both agriculture and Catholicism.[1] As more Europeans settled in Canada and on the traditional lands of Indigenous Peoples, the authorities saw they needed an effective means to ensure that the most fertile land was available to European farmers. The development of the reserve system met this need.

There was no consistent formula for designating land to a band. For example, of the Numbered Treaties, which were signed between the Canadian government and various Indigenous groups between 1871 and 1921, Treaties 1 (1871, between Canada and the Anishinaabeg and Swampy Cree of southern Manitoba) and 2 (1871, between Canada and the Anishinaabeg of southern Manitoba) used the ratio of 160 acres for every family of five. Treaties 3 to 11 (except for Treaty 5, which used the same ratio as Treaties 1 and 2) allocated 640 acres per family of five. In British Columbia, the ratio was an average of 20 acres granted per family. A band may have more than one reserve, and the reserves may or may not be contiguous.[2]

Because underlying title to the land remains vested with the Crown, reserve lands are not fee simple and are not subject to seizure under legal process. Thus, Indian reserve land cannot be sold, except to the Crown, and does not appreciate in value the same way that property held in fee simple does for other Canadians. This makes it very difficult for a Status Indian to borrow funds. Crown ownership also affects how reserve lands can be developed. Most reserve housing is owned by the federal government.

The Albatross Rears Its Ugly Head in Real Estate

I was recently looking at purchasing a property on the reserve of a community that has a great track record of developing reserve property. I made an offer with the realtor, who said I should include "subject to financing" and "subject to being able to secure insurance" clauses in my offer. I agreed, and we proceeded with the offer. I began the process of trying to borrow money to purchase the property, which was taking longer than I thought necessary. My realtor suggested that while waiting for the financing to come through, I check on getting insurance for the property. I went to a local insurance broker with experience insuring properties on this reserve and was told I couldn't get insurance because the property was not going to be my principal residence. I did more research and discovered that insurance prices are pretty high on reserves. Because bands fall under the *Indian Act*, housing bylaws may not conform to the insurance agencies' expectations for construction and infrastructure standards. All this to say, it makes the insurance more expensive.

Looking at issues such as property seizure, access to capital markets, and even how development can happen on reserve reveals that the system in place for those without self-government agreements hamstrings their ability to participate in the economy.

The Government of Canada's self-government policy has been developed, tested, and refined over time. It is designed to give communities decision-making power to manage their lands, business opportunities, social programs, and more. Communities such as Westbank First Nation offer an example of how to use self-government power to make laws that address the restrictions of the *Indian Act* and deliver better outcomes for the Nation.[3] Because of its self-government agreement, the Westbank First Nation's lands are governed by community laws, not the *Indian Act*, giving the Nation "full jurisdictional control over its Lands and resources."[4] The Westbank First Nation Land Registry Regulations works in conjunction with the Land Rules established in the Westbank First Nation Constitution and offers benefits such as reduction of lending risk, reduced cost of business, and security and certainty to investors and developers. A drive through Westbank First Nation or Tsawwassen First Nation lands will show you the result of their hard work. You will see all manner of investing and land development, including residential real estate, hotels, restaurants, recreation, light industrial buildings, commercial, and retail centres.

The Westbank First Nation example alone should compel Canada to enter into more self-government agreements with all the bands that don't have such agreements sooner rather than later. Let's put our foot on the gas pedal and finish the job!

{ 6 }

Laws of General Application Apply

IF YOU WERE to take the time to read through a self-government agreement, you may notice references to the "laws of general application" that continue to apply. Some examples of these laws are the *Criminal Code*, the *Canadian Charter of Rights and Freedoms*, and the *Environmental Protection Act*.

A major component of legislative authority included in a negotiated settlement (for example, in a self-government agreement or treaty) is that Indigenous governments can make their own laws—as long as they meet or exceed what other governments are doing. For example, the Nisga'a Nation could pass its own forest practices legislation as long as it met or exceeded provincial and federal standards. The Government of Canada's *Nisga'a Final Agreement 2001 Annual Report* reflects this wording: "Now that the Nisga'a Nation has ownership and control over its forests, it is concentrating on managing the resource. The Nisga'a

Final Agreement stipulates that Nisga'a forest practices meet or exceed British Columbia forest practice legislation. NLG [Nisga'a Lisims Government] is committed to achieving this goal while providing consistent, sustainable employment for forestry workers."[1]

Justice

Many self-government agreements include a justice component with the objective of being responsible to the needs and priorities of a particular nation. Chapter 12 of the Nisga'a Final Agreement[2] provides the ability to create a police board, police services, community correction services, and a court. Community correction services are delivered to the Nation under federal and provincial legislation in accordance with generally accepted standards, along with being consistent with the needs and priorities of the Nation. If the Nation were to establish a court, chapter 12 requires that the court be established applying generally recognized principles of judicial fairness, independence, and impartiality.

The Anishinabek Nation Governance Agreement (2022)[3] takes a slightly different direction than the Nisga'a Final Agreement. Chapter 6 of the Anishinabek Nation Governance Agreement focuses on enforcement and adjudication laws. It provides the ability to establish services, including restorative justice or mediation, for the voluntary settlement of disputes, in addition to traditional Anishinaabe processes. The Agreement also allows for Anishinaabe sanctions to deal with alleged offences under First Nation or Anishinabek Nation laws. The importance of the Anishinaabe culture is seen in section 6.4 of the Agreement, which provides that "each First Nation and the Anishinabek Nation under this Agreement may provide for Anishinaabe sanctions that are consistent with Anishinaabe customs, culture, traditions and values, provided that such sanctions are proportionate to the seriousness of the offence and are not imposed on an offender without his or her consent."[4] This Agreement is not considered a final agreement. Future negotiations in areas of administration of justice, policing, and others are outlined further in chapter 13 of the Agreement.

The Westbank First Nation Self-Government Agreement is much less detailed in the area of justice. Similar to the Nisga'a and Anishinabek agreements, Westbank First Nation's agreement provides the ability to establish laws and enforce them.[5] It also recognizes that there may be future negotiations around social programs, creating courts, and other areas of governance.

Another similarity between all three agreements is that federal and provincial legislation still applies to the Nation and its governance unless otherwise provided for in the Agreement.

… { 7 }

Traditional Leadership Is Tied to Community

AS WITH most aspects of life for Indigenous Peoples in Canada, the introduction of the *Indian Act* in 1876 injected a seismic shift into governance. Prior to the *Indian Act*, Nations had their own traditional governing structures and protocols. Hereditary Chiefs could hold many different positions and have different powers within a community, including leadership, territory, and land. Each Indigenous community had their own decision-making processes on the traditional leadership of its community, many following a matriarchal line. The power of traditional or hereditary leaders was frequently passed from one generation to another through cultural laws.

The introduction of European-style elections by the *Indian Act* threatened the continuity of traditional governing structures—the very backbone of each Nation. Canada desired a more recognizable way for Indigenous communities to communicate with the government and represent their respective Nations, and so implemented an Elected Chief and Councils. This policy set out to eradicate the concept of Hereditary Chiefs, something westernized democracy was not familiar with. The traditional governance structures of many Nations were part of a productive and highly evolved society pre-European contact, and many lost the traditions of these structures throughout Canada's history, including the undermining of women and Elders in leadership roles.

Under the *Indian Act*, Nations that had thrived and survived on their own terms before European contact became "bands." Each band is allowed one Elected Chief and one Elected Councillor for every 100 band members, with a minimum of 2 and no more than 12 councillors per band.[1] These elected officials are ultimately accountable to the federal government and federal policy. A key takeaway about the *Indian Act* electoral process is that the Chief and Council are elected by their people but are accountable to the federal government because the federal government controls their mandate and funding (which pays their salaries). The concept is fraught with potential pitfalls.

An Elected Chief and Council are responsible for delivering federal government programming for health care, housing, and education on reserve. Their responsibilities are confined, or should be confined, to reserve operations.[2]

Where I come from, Hereditary Chiefs are responsible for the Nation's Traditional Territory (the geographic area identified as the land that a Nation and/or its ancestors traditionally occupied or used). They make decisions about lands and resources and are responsible for the collective community.

When, in 2019–20, the news first hit of protests by some Wet'suwet'en First Nation Hereditary Chiefs over a Coastal GasLink pipeline project that was to cut through the Nation's territory, it sparked a sudden public interest in Hereditary Chiefs. The number of visitors to Indigenous Corporate Training Inc.'s 2016 blog post "Hereditary Chief Definition and 5 FAQs"[3] skyrocketed, and news outlets across the country came calling for more information on Hereditary Chiefs, how their roles and responsibilities differed from Elected Chiefs, and how a Nation could have both.

An underlying issue in the Wet'suwet'en situation was that the consultation focused on the Elected Chiefs along the route. The pipeline narrative was that Coastal GasLink had signed agreements with all the bands, meaning those institutions created under the *Indian Act*. A number of Hereditary Chiefs believed they were not consulted or not adequately consulted and protested the construction of the pipeline across their traditional lands. We take a deeper dive into whom governments and corporations need to talk to in chapter 16, "Free, Prior, and Informed Consent Must Be Obtained."

A Three-Part Story About Hereditary Leadership

I am frequently asked who outranks whom when both Hereditary and Elected Band Chiefs are present in a community. My answer is a three-part story about hereditary leadership.

A client group and I visited a community to attend a presentation from a Hereditary Chief, as we had the same question: Who outranks whom? With the Hereditary Chief was a quiet, elderly lady wearing a hand-knit sweater. She sat by the refreshment table, drinking tea while the Hereditary Chief gave a great presentation.

Then it was our turn to ask questions, which he graciously answered.

The first question was about who makes decisions in the community, the Elected Chief or Hereditary Chiefs? The Hereditary Chief answered that in his community, there were several Hereditary Chiefs and one Elected Band Chief. For decisions about their territory, lands, and resources, each of the Hereditary Chiefs were responsible for a portion of that territory. So, if a forestry company wanted to cut down trees in an area, the company would need to talk to the Hereditary Chief who had the rights and responsibilities to that specific portion of the broader territory. If a pipeline company wanted to put a pipeline across the entire territory, they'd have to talk to all the Hereditary Chiefs. That answer gave us some good insight.

The next question was in three parts: "How do the Hereditary Chiefs get along with the Elected Band Chief, and does the Band Chief know that the resource companies have to speak to the Hereditary Chiefs, and does the Band Chief respect their decisions?" The answer will give you some good insights.

The Hereditary Chief explained that, yes, the Band Chief is aware of their respective jurisdictional accountabilities. When the Band Chief listens to and respects their decisions, both sets of leadership get along great. If the Elected Chief does not listen, the Hereditary Chiefs can, between all of them and with the support of their communities, make sure that the Band Chief is not a successful candidate in the next election.

"How do you learn to be a Hereditary Chief?" was the last question asked in this meeting.

The Hereditary Chief said, "It's a great question." But before he answered, he called out, "Hey, Auntie, can you come up here, please?" And Auntie, who had been quietly sipping tea, walked up to the front and stood behind him, looking over his shoulder. "So, this is my auntie. A while ago she gave me my chieftainship and largely taught me how to be a chief, and today I am able to do that and make decisions. And if I am ever stuck, I go to Auntie."

And then he said, "Thank you, Auntie," and she sat down again without ever saying a word.

So, we went into the day thinking, "We've got to talk to the Band Chief." But by the middle of the day, we were thinking, "We've got to talk to these Hereditary Chiefs about lands and resources." And by the end of the day, we were all thinking, "Auntie! She's the power broker!"

Restoring Traditional Leadership

Self-government provides the opportunity for Nations to restore, if possible, their traditional leadership. For some Nations, much has been lost because of *Indian Act* policies that prohibited cultural protocols and traditions deemed anti-assimilation. Given the passage of time and the impact of living under the *Indian Act* for over 150 years, restoring traditional leadership in today's world could require modifications. As then Chief Sophie Pierre of the Ktunaxa/Kinbasket Tribal Council (now called the Ktunaxa Nation Council) noted in a presentation to the British Columbia Treaty Commission:

> One of the most difficult realities that we face is that our previous method of governance, the Ktunaxa

governance, has been largely lost through the legislated restriction of First Nations cultural practices within Canada. As we redevelop our governance system, we face an enormous challenge [...] we have to consider how to blend, first of all, our relationship with and within Canada and British Columbia, secondly, community comfort levels and the new distribution of powers and authorities and expectations created under the last century of governance under the *Indian Act* and lastly, elements of historical government structures and powers that have withstood the passage of time. We need to be creative on how we blend those three areas.[4]

The big takeaway in this discussion is that the roles and responsibilities of traditional leaders are tied to the collective community and not to an outside agency. If we are going to continue to dismantle the *Indian Act*, we, as Canadians, have to create a space where communities can have conversations about governance, free of outside influence. The choice is with the communities: We must let communities decide if Chiefs should be elected, traditional/hereditary, a blend of both, or something completely different.

Agreements Involving Hereditary Chiefs

As someone who, at the time of writing, is on the verge of becoming a Hereditary Chief, I must show my bias and take the opportunity to include a few examples of agreements that involve Hereditary Chiefs.

The Maa-nulth First Nations Final Agreement (2011)[5] requires that each of the five Maa-nulth First Nations on the West Coast of Vancouver Island have a constitution that provides for a government that is democratically and financially accountable to the Maa-nulth-aht. At the discretion of each Maa-nulth First Nation, its constitution may provide for the appointment of ḥaw̓iiḥ (Hereditary Chiefs) into its government structure as long as the majority of representatives within each Maa-nulth First Nation government will be elected.

The Huu-ay-aht First Nations is one of five signatories to the Maa-nulth First Nations Final Agreement. They see the blended leadership as a strength: "With full control over these undisputed lands owned in fee simple, our Nation is able to govern the lands under our own laws. Seeking to leverage this strength, Huu-ay-aht First Nations Council and Hereditary Chiefs (ḥaw̓iiḥ) have been actively seeking opportunities to engage in responsible and sustainable economic development in order to forward the Huu-ay-aht vision of working together to establish a healthy, prosperous, and self-sustaining community."[6]

Another example is the Ta'an Kwach'an Council Self-Government Agreement (2002).[7] For this Agreement, the Ta'an Kwäch'än Council was represented by its Hereditary Chief, Glenn Grady, as signatory to the Agreement. The Ta'an Kwäch'än Council, located in the Yukon, also referenced that its decision-making structures were based on a moiety system[8] form of social organization, and the Council wanted to maintain these structures. In keeping with its desire for a blended leadership, the Board of the Ta'an Kwäch'än Council consists of one Chief, one Deputy Chief, and nine Family Directors from the Traditional Families named in section 8 of its constitution.[9]

Again, it's a community choice whether to include Hereditary Chiefs, if any, or instead go with a more democratic model of governance. I say "if any" as some communities don't have Hereditary Chiefs.

The 'Namgis Nation office is located in Alert Bay, BC, the place of my birth, and the Nation is currently working towards a self-government agreement. Many of my family and friends live there or are from there. The Nation, on an article on its website titled "The Journey to Gwayile'las," states the following:

> 'Namgis Chief and Council has come together with 'Namgis Hereditary leaders to start the important process of creating a new system of governance for the 'Namgis Nation—a system where 'Namgis elected and traditional leaders will work together to implement 'Namgis self-determination, self-government and self-reliance following Gwayile'las—"Our Way."
>
> We are creating this new system because we heard from 'Namgis members that blended governance shared between elected and traditional leaders is important to you. From 1998 to 2013, 'Namgis was involved in the BC Treaty Process. During this time a Draft Constitution was developed by the Treaty Caucus—including Hereditary Chiefs. This Constitution would have replaced the existing Band Council structure with a new structure which included representation of Hereditary Chiefs.[10]

We can see from these three examples how some Nations are incorporating their hereditary leadership into new self-governing systems.

{ 8 }

Nations Have the Right to Choose Their People

LONG BEFORE the arrival of Europeans, the establishing of Confederation, and the imposition of the *Indian Act*, Indigenous communities decided who their people were based on cultural protocols, clan and kinship systems, and family structures, among other considerations. There weren't bands or reserves or status, so there was no concept of people living "off reserve" or being "non-status."

When the *Indian Act* was consolidated in 1876 and assimilation did not proceed as anticipated, the federal government began to tighten control. By the late 1940s, the federal government exercised formidable control over the lives of Indians as defined by the *Indian Act* specifically, and Indigenous Peoples more broadly.

In 1951, the *Indian Act* underwent a significant revision. Some of the more stringent rules, such as the ban on cultural ceremonies and the pursuit of land claims, were repealed. Other rules, such as the criteria for status, were tightened. Indian Affairs created a centralized Indian Register in Ottawa to determine who was legally considered an "Indian" and, therefore, worthy of status. Bands lost what power they had over their membership. The Indian Register created and controlled a centralized list of names on band lists. If your name was on that list, you were a Status Indian in the eyes of the federal government.

Being a registered or Status Indian became synonymous with band membership, the right to live on reserve, and access to programs and services. Those without status were forced to leave their families and communities and live elsewhere, most frequently in urban centres, without support. Women, in particular, were victimized by the narrowing criteria of status.

The targeting of women for exclusion from status and band membership was extreme in the 1951 amendments. Under section 12(1)(b), male Indians who married out (married a non-Indian woman) kept their status, and their wives and children of that marriage gained status. If an Indian woman married out, she lost her status, her children and her spouse were denied status, and she and her immediate family had to leave the reserve. If she later divorced or became a widow, she did not regain status, so she was not allowed to return to the reserve, where her extended family and community likely lived. This expulsion set the stage for the high number of missing and murdered Indigenous women.

That non-Indian women who married a Status Indian man acquired status, as did their children, was an added insult to Indian women.

As a result of the *Canadian Charter of Rights and Freedoms*, and protests and legal actions by Indigenous women, the federal government removed some of the *Indian Act*'s more discriminatory policies in 1985 (but non-Indian women who gained status through marriage before 1985 did not lose their status). One significant amendment gave bands the right to create their own membership codes (section 10) or maintain membership regulation with the Indian Registrar (section 11). The majority chose section 10.

Political and financial considerations impacted the criteria for some membership codes. It was not uncommon for codes to further restrict membership and force more people from the reserves, breaking up families and ties to culture, ceremony, and access to ancestral lands.[1]

It's important to note that some bands use the term "membership," whereas others use "citizenship." There is a small but mighty distinction between the two. "Membership" is *Indian Act* terminology. For many communities, "citizenship" is the word of choice.

Self-Government and Citizenship

The UN Declaration on the Rights of Indigenous Peoples supports the right to choose who your people are and what governance you will use.

Article 33

1 Indigenous peoples have the right to determine their own identity or membership in accordance with their customs and traditions. This does not impair the right of Indigenous individuals to obtain citizenship of the States in which they live.

2 Indigenous peoples have the right to determine the structures and to select the membership of their institutions in accordance with their own procedures.²

Citizenship codes are typically based on traditional protocols, family, kinship, and a belief that people, land, and the environment define belonging. They are generally written to include those who were forced out of the community by *Indian Act* politics of exclusion—in other words, people who have been declared non-status because of marriage or adoption, or some other *Indian Act* criteria. These individuals are a large, invisible portion of Indigenous Peoples populations who often contend with poverty, estrangement from their cultures, and political disenfranchisement from their community. They are the ones who fall through all the social safety nets that are supposed to be in place to look after "Indians, and Lands reserved for the Indians." They are victims of the restrictions and have far fewer benefits when it comes to taxes, education, and housing.

Self-government agreements have allowed Nations to outline their citizenship rules. Oftentimes the details of citizenship are contained in a Nation's constitution. The constitution of the Haida Nation, for example, states that all people of Haida ancestry are citizens of the Haida Nation and that adoption of a person without Haida ancestry by a person/family of Haida ancestry does not grant that person hereditary or aboriginal rights to the land nor Haida citizenship.³ The Haida have included an honorary designation in their constitution called a "Citizen of Haida

Gwaii." This may be conferred on a person not of Haida ancestry and, as with adoption, does not grant any hereditary or aboriginal rights to land or citizenship.[4]

The Gwich'in Comprehensive Land Claim Agreement (1992),[5] on the other hand, defines a Gwich'in as a person of Gwich'in (also referred to as Loucheux) ancestry who resided in, or used and occupied the settlement area on or before December 31, 1921, or is a descendant of such person; or who was adopted as a minor, by a Gwich'in person, or is the descendant of a person so adopted. To be eligible to be enrolled, a person must be a Canadian citizen and be a Gwich'in. In situations where someone is not eligible, they can be enrolled if that person is "a Canadian citizen of aboriginal ancestry, resident in the settlement area, and accepted by the Gwich'in at any time following the date of settlement legislation."[6]

Speaking of kinship, while I am writing this book, I am also planning my inaugural Potlatch as a future Kwakwaka'wakw Hereditary Chief. This Potlatch will confirm both my name and my seat in our house (of government), provided that I follow the correct procedures and receive support from the Chiefs and the community. Guests will show their support by accepting the gifts that I distribute to them at the appropriate time during the ceremony. The term "Potlatch" comes from Chinook trade jargon and means "gift-giving ceremony."

One of the important things I have to consider when planning a Potlatch is the names that will be given. This ceremonial act of self-determination, choosing, and giving names during the Potlatch is an important part of self-determination and was based on teachings from my father, close family, relatives, other community members, and my experiences at other Potlatches.

The first step is to get in touch with a family member who has a vast knowledge of available names and to determine which name should be given to which individual. These names will be given to our relatives at the appropriate time during the Potlatch. This act will fulfill our obligation and establish their membership and standing within the community. It will also ensure that they, and all Nation citizens, know that they are loved, cared for, and have a place in this world.

{ 9 }

Nations Determine Their Financial Checks and Balances

BEFORE WE discuss financial accountability and transparency, I want to acknowledge that, yes, there is corruption in some First Nations communities.[1] However, the vast majority of Band Councils are financially transparent and accountable.

Back in 2014–15, a few bands generated considerable notoriety for the magnitude of the salaries that Chiefs were paying themselves while community members lived in poverty.[2] The ensuing media frenzy provided fodder for pundits who were quick to promote the idea that all Chiefs were dishonest. This did a vast disservice to Indigenous relations across the country.

The federal government passed the *First Nations Financial Transparency Act*[3] in 2013 to strengthen the financial accountability and transparency of Elected Chiefs and

Councils. The Act was passed without any consultation with First Nations.

"About us without us."

The *First Nations Financial Transparency Act* requires public disclosure of the audited consolidated financial statements and the schedules of remuneration and expenses of the Chief.[4] Those who were not compliant had their band administration funding withheld. The majority were compliant, but some Chiefs objected to being ordered to publish the band's consolidated financial statement publicly because doing so put band businesses that competed in the open market at a competitive disadvantage. In December 2015, the Minister of Indigenous and Northern Affairs Canada (INAC) issued a statement indicating that the department had stopped all discretionary compliance measures related to the *First Nations Financial Transparency Act*, was re-instating funding withheld from First Nations under those measures, and was suspending any court actions against First Nations who had not complied with the Act.[5]

Because Elected Band Chiefs are accountable to the federal government (the entity paying their compensation) and not the people who elected them, if a band member raises concerns about accountability or transparency, they leave themselves open for reprisals, such as those related to access to housing, health, or education programs and services. The federal government does not get involved in the internal workings of bands, so if the Band Council declines to be transparent with a band member about its operations, there is no help to enforce disclosure of information.

For Indigenous leaders to criticize the federal government can likewise be risky. The experience of former National Chief of the Assembly of First Nations (AFN) Matthew Coon Come demonstrated that an outspoken national Chief will have his funding cut.

As Bill Curry reported in the *Globe and Mail*, "Mr. Coon Come attracted international attention in 2001 when he told a United Nations forum that the Canadian government was racist and used 'lethal force' toward its aboriginal population. By the end of his first and only term, Jean Chrétien's Liberal government had cut the AFN's budget to $6-million from $19-million."[6]

Financial Accountability and Transparency Under Self-Government

There are requirements for accountability mechanisms when the federal government and an Indigenous Nation sign a self-government agreement. According to Government of Canada policy, "Mechanisms to ensure political accountability must be developed and ratified by the Aboriginal group concerned, and set out in an internal constitution so that they are transparent to all members, and to others who deal with the Aboriginal governments or institutions."[7]

When a community decides to move away from being wards of the state and return to self-government, the decision begins a process of discussions to develop the Nation's constitution or resurrect its cultural code of conduct or other governance code. During these meetings, the checks and balances for accountability and transparency will be built into the constitution. For example, the Squamish Nation is involved in a two-year process in which Squamish people and the community will help draft the Nation's constitution, "deciding our way of being a nation."[8]

Other Nations have self-government agreements that build financial accountability into their constitutions. The Tłı̨chǫ government in the Northwest Territories has the Tłı̨chǫ Land Claims and Self-Government Agreement (2005). Its section 7.1.2(c) stipulates that the Tłı̨chǫ Constitution shall provide "a system of political and financial accountability to Tłı̨chǫ Citizens."[9] The Tłı̨chǫ Constitution[10] broadly states that it is accountable to the Tłı̨chǫ, and the Tłı̨chǫ Government Administrative Policy and Procedures details the use of generally accepted accounting principles.[11]

Systems under the *Indian Act* and under self-government may look the same from the outside, but they are very different. Under the *Indian Act* system, a Nation's leadership reports to the federal government, who sets the mandate. Under self government, the citizens of the community set the mandate, and the Nation's government is accountable to the citizens it serves. The Nation's citizens determine the checks and balances, not the federal government.

"Everything about us by us."

{ 10 }

The Fiduciary Duty Diminishes

THERE ARE over 630 First Nations communities in Canada. The federal government established each one as an autonomous entity and, under the *Indian Act*, determines, on a yearly basis, how much money will be available, when and how it will be made available, and for what purposes. This format gives First Nation governments little opportunity to make long-range strategic plans or set their own priorities. This excerpt from the Government of Canada "Budget Management Principles" webpage outlines funding principles:

> ISC [Indigenous Services Canada] works collaboratively with partners to improve access to high quality services for First Nations, Inuit and Métis.
> ISC budget management decisions seek to:
> - *respond to* needs and emerging pressures
> - sustain ongoing service delivery

- optimize funding and benefits to Indigenous communities
- implement government priorities[1] [emphasis added]

To me, "respond to" rather than "meets" tells the whole story of underfunding of Indigenous Peoples on reserves. When you examine Indigenous Services Canada's response to the need for services and programs for education, emergency management, governance, health, housing, infrastructure, land and economic development, social supports, and water, it becomes clear that before funding is allocated, there needs to be lower levels of education, poorer health, and inadequate housing on reserves to respond to. If you want to learn more about funding, *Expert Analysis: Federal Funding and First Nations in Canada* is a report prepared at the request of a First Nation and their legal team for a matter before the Supreme Court of Canada.[2] It's an interesting read.

Although the federal government provides separate program funding to each community, the responsibility for delivering these services is left to the communities themselves. This format is fraught with issues, one of which is a lack of oversight, which the federal government appears to address by requiring excessive reporting on each nation's part. A 2011 *Status Report of the Auditor General of Canada to the House of Commons* notes:

> In 2002, we looked at the amount of reporting required of First Nations by federal organizations. We estimated that four federal organizations together required about 168 reports annually from each First

Nations reserve. We found that many of the reports were unnecessary and were not in fact used by the federal organizations. We followed up on this issue in 2006. At that time, we found that federal departments had made little progress on meeting our recommendations to reduce reporting requirements. In our 2006 follow-up audit, we reported that INAC's officials told us that the Department obtained more than 60,000 reports a year from over 600 First Nations communities.[3]

Many communities are small, some with fewer than 50 residents living on reserve. These smaller, remote communities sometimes lack the expertise required to administer programs and services typically provided by federal, provincial, and municipal governments. An inordinate amount of time is consumed filling in reports that may never be read by the ministry involved.

The excessive reporting regime does little more than confirm compliance with the terms and conditions of the funding agreement. Excessive reporting neither measures the effectiveness of the programs in closing socio-economic gaps nor provides effective policy and program guidance. It seems clear from this report that the gaps are not closing.

Funding Under Self-Government

Every government requires and receives revenue to fund the cost of governing. Non-Indigenous governments rely on funds from various sources such as transfers, taxes, fees, and levies from resource development. These funds pay for the services delivered, such as health care, education, infrastructure, policing, and so on. Self-governing Indigenous Nations are no different.

The federal government has a historical and ongoing, constitutionally protected fiduciary duty to Indigenous Peoples. Recognizing the right to self-government does not end that relationship. As Indigenous Nations return to self-government, self-determination, and self-reliance and assume greater autonomy, the fiduciary responsibility will lessen but not disappear. The government is committed to renewing fiscal arrangements with Indigenous Peoples under self-government: "Fiscal arrangements detail the ongoing funding relationship between the Indigenous government, Canada and, where applicable, provincial or territorial governments. The arrangement provides funding that supports the operations of the Indigenous government to effectively deliver programs and services to its members on an ongoing basis. These fiscal agreements generally have a 5 year term."[4]

The fiscal arrangements between Canada and self-governing Indigenous governments should be guided by the following principles set out in Canada's Collaborative Self-Government Fiscal Policy:

20.1. Sufficiency: Indigenous Governments should have access to sufficient fiscal resources to fulfill their responsibilities and address associated expenditure needs.

20.2. Access to public services: Members of the communities represented by the Indigenous Government should have access to programs and services that are reasonably comparable to those available to other Canadians in similar circumstances.

20.3. Equitable treatment: Fiscal arrangements should provide for equitable treatment of Indigenous Governments across Canada, taking into account their differing circumstances.

20.4. Self-determination and autonomy: An Indigenous Government has the autonomy to set its own priorities, allocate its fiscal resources and determine how to deliver culturally-appropriate programs and services.

20.5. Stability, predictability and flexibility: Fiscal arrangements should be reasonably stable and predictable over time, while providing sufficient flexibility to address changing circumstances.

20.6. Transparency: Fiscal arrangements should be transparent and open to public view.

20.7. Efficiency and effectiveness: Fiscal arrangements should seek opportunities for the effective and efficient delivery of programs and services, while recognizing diseconomies of scale and demographic features.

20.8. Sustainability and affordability: Fiscal arrangements should be sustainable and affordable for governments.

20.9. Accountability: Fiscal arrangements should promote accountability through clarity of roles and responsibilities and sound public administration.

20.10. Simplicity: Fiscal arrangements should be relatively simple and straightforward to implement.[5]

Within current self-government agreements we see the application of these principles. The obligations of the federal and provincial governments for programs and funding shall continue on the same basis as for the other Indigenous Peoples in Canada. This is contained in the James Bay and Northern Quebec Agreement (s. 2.12); Anishinabek Nation Governance Agreement (s. 8.13); Westbank First Nation Self-Government Agreement (Financial Arrangements); and Sioux Valley Dakota Nation Governance Agreement and Tripartite Governance Agreement (2014) (s. 64.02).[6]

Self-government agreements are a political solution to a legal problem.

The legal problem is that Canada has a fiduciary duty to look after "Indians, and Lands reserved for the Indians" under the *Indian Act*. The trustee (the federal government), in this case, faces many challenges in administering the Act. How then, can we get out of this legal problem? Entering into negotiations and changing the relationship through those discussions, moving towards self-government and dismantling the *Indian Act*, gives us that opportunity.

This is where the *Indian Act Amendment and Replacement Act*[7] comes into play. In the conclusion of the *Tenth Annual (2024) Statutory Report Pursuant to Section 2 of the Indian Act Amendment and Replacement Act, Statutes of Canada, Chapter 38, 2014*, we see a gradual transfer of departmental responsibility to Indigenous control, which is a political solution to a legal problem of recognizing and affirming the right to self-determination. You can read the text here:

Indigenous Services Canada's legislated mandate of closing socio-economic gaps and the gradual transfer of departmental responsibilities to Indigenous control is, ultimately, about recognizing and affirming Indigenous Peoples' inherent right to self-determination. It is essential that work to meet this mandate respects the distinct needs and mandates of First Nations, Inuit, and Métis, and that it upholds treaty and Aboriginal rights, and federal obligations.

Indigenous Services Canada will continue to work with Indigenous partners on refining and increasing Indigenous access to quality services that are essential to closing socio-economic gaps. The department will do this through co-developed initiatives that build community capacity and support to the unique needs of Indigenous Peoples, and we will continue to actively work towards the shared objective of transferring the full responsibility of design and delivery of culturally appropriate services to Indigenous control.

Achieving progress on transfer, as well as closing socio-economic gaps, will require continued investments to ensure future sustainability. Experience has shown that investing in services where Indigenous governments and organizations played a key role in their design and delivery leads to better outcomes for all Indigenous groups. In supporting self-determination, we can have an immediate positive impact on the closing of socio-economic gaps between Indigenous Peoples and non-Indigenous people in Canada.[8]

With the *Indian Act Amendment and Replacement Act* and as demonstrated in its accompanying report, the Government of Canada is progressing in the transfer of responsibilities and closing socio-economic gaps, and it will continue to fund this work, which will lead to better outcomes for everyone. If we do more of this faster, along with taking on other ideas about Indigenous self-governance in this book, we can really make positive changes for Canada and Canadians.

{ 11 }

Tax Is Included

THE IDEA that "Indians don't pay taxes" is a hot-button issue for many and is one of the enduring myths about Indigenous Peoples. So, before we dig into taxes and self-government, it's essential to dispel the myth.

Status Indians are subject to the same tax rules as other Canadian residents unless their income is eligible for the tax exemption under section 87 of the *Indian Act*, which states that "personal property of an Indian or a Band situated on a reserve" is tax exempt. "Personal property" includes goods, services, and income. Employment income earned by a Status Indian through employment on a reserve is tax exempt. Income earned off reserve is not tax exempt; non-Status Indians are not eligible for this tax exemption.

The purpose of this exemption is to preserve the entitlements of Indians to their reserve lands and to ensure that the use of their property on their reserve lands is not eroded by taxes. From the Canada Revenue Agency website:

- A tax exemption for Indian property situated on reserves has existed since before Confederation.

- The Supreme Court of Canada has stated that this exemption is linked to the protection of reserve land and property.

- The Court has concluded that the purpose of the exemption is to make sure tax does not erode the use of Indian property on reserves.

- The Court has indicated that this tax exemption is not intended to remedy the economically disadvantaged position of Aboriginal people in Canada or bring economic benefits to them.[1]

Also, based on Supreme Court decisions, Status Indian property not situated on a reserve will generally be subject to tax just like property held by other Canadians.

Since Inuit, Métis, and non-Status Indians are not subject to the *Indian Act*, they are not eligible for the Indian tax exemption on income earned.[2] This exemption under the *Indian Act* benefits few Indigenous Peoples. It is restricted not just to Status Indians but specifically to Status Indians living, working, or having access to a reserve. What it does create is an inability for Indigenous leadership of Nations to tax their communities in order to provide local funding of band services and programs.

Taxes Under Self-Government

Under self-government, the decision about how, what, and if to tax is up to each Nation, but stepping away from the *Indian Act* means an end to tax exemptions. Changes in governance structure resulting from self-government agreements gives more jurisdiction and control to bands over their lands and grants them legal authority to tax developments and individuals on reserve lands. "As of 2020, approximately 30% of 624 First Nations have established First Nation taxation on their reserve lands."[3]

Under the Tsawwassen First Nation Final Agreement (2009),[4] the Nation gained direct taxation powers in respect of property tax along with personal sales tax and income tax. The exemptions for personal sales tax and income tax were kept in place for the first 8 and 12 years, respectively, but those have now expired. The Tsawwassen First Nation's financial statements for the 2023–24 fiscal year show it generated almost $33 million in revenue, mainly through property taxes, developmental levies, and lease revenue. But as a growing Nation, it will also have increased costs. Through these revenues, it intends to provide more programs and services directly to the Tsawwassen community.[5]

Another option for taxation under self-government is tax-sharing agreements with the Government of Canada. An example is the First Nations Goods and Services Tax (FNGST). FNGST can be imposed by a Band Council on lands it governs and the same basic rules of GST/HST apply. The tax is payable by all individuals, including Status Indian purchasers. Where FNGST is imposed, the GST or federal portion of the HST does not apply to purchases. There are currently 39 First Nations collecting FNGST for purchases made on their lands.

Taxation is an important topic. I expand on it in chapter 15, "Self-Reliance and Economic Reconciliation Can Begin with Small Actions."

{ 12 }

Indigenous Rights Include Language Rights

THE UN DECLARATION recognizes the right for Indigenous Peoples to revitalize, use, and transmit their languages, and it calls for federal governments to ensure this right is protected.

Article 11

1. Indigenous peoples have the right to practise and revitalize their cultural traditions and customs. This includes the right to maintain, protect and develop the past, present and future manifestations of their cultures, such as archaeological and historical sites, artefacts, designs, ceremonies, technologies and visual and performing arts and literature.

2. States shall provide redress through effective mechanisms, which may include restitution, developed in conjunction with indigenous peoples, with respect

> to their cultural, intellectual, religious and spiritual property taken without their free, prior and informed consent or in violation of their laws, traditions and customs.[1]

During the era of residential schools (between the 1870s and late 1990s), an estimated 150,000 children were removed from their families and communities and placed in the schools.[2] While interned in the schools, the children were forbidden to speak their home language; if they did, they often were subjected to horrific forms of punishment and other abuse. When the children returned home for holidays, they were frequently too traumatized to converse in their language. And when they had children of their own, they frequently did not teach or encourage them to speak their home language, in part because their fluency had been impacted, in part because they feared their children would suffer the same punishment, and in part because they believed their children needed fluency in the dominant language. Multiply that scenario through the generations, and we have a 2021 statistic that just 13.1 per cent of people who identify as Indigenous can speak an Indigenous language (this number is down from 15 per cent in 2016).[3]

Language is the foundation of a culture. For Indigenous oral societies, words hold knowledge, stories, songs, dances, protocols, family histories, and connections. Languages also often hold a community's customary laws that were eroded by the policies of the *Indian Act*. For some communities, as they move towards a return to self-government, this loss of laws and systems of governance means they may not have that knowledge to draw upon.

Language holds knowledge. It is an invaluable source of information about the history of the natural environment, climate and climate changes over time, plants, and animals. It is an irretrievable body of knowledge. Science, medicine, governments, and resource planners all rely in part on Indigenous Traditional Knowledge and are impacted when that irreplaceable storehouse of traditional environmental knowledge is gone. Each language that dies equals the loss of a cultural treasure.

When a language dies so does the link to the cultural and historical past. Without that crucial connection to their linguistic and cultural history, people lose their sense of identity and belonging. Research has proven that learning and having the ability to speak an Indigenous language improves self-esteem, lowers the rates of death by suicide, promotes academic success, and strengthens the connection between Indigenous Peoples and their culture.

Indigenous students are increasingly attending school away from their territories and growing up learning the dominant and common language used in their region, such as English or French. The migration of young people to urban centres for education, housing, and employment opportunities is negatively impacting the preservation of Indigenous languages. According to Statistics Canada,

> over two-thirds (67.8%) of the 183,790 First Nations people who reported they could speak an Indigenous language lived on reserve in 2021, highlighting the importance of community in language retention. Since most on-reserve residents are First Nations people, it can be easier to learn and retain an Indigenous language when hearing it spoken and used every day. In 2021,

> 39.8% of First Nations people living on reserve could speak an Indigenous language, compared with 8.0% of those living off reserve.[4]

The preservation and revitalization of languages, traditions, and cultures is a high priority for Indigenous Peoples, just as it is for other communities. Moves towards self-governance allow communities to prioritize their languages, traditions, and cultures.

The Yukon government and a committee of First Nations Chiefs, in 2022, established the First Nation School Board (FNSB), which allows First Nations communities in the territory to assume greater authority and control over how children are educated. Board-run schools continue to follow the BC curriculum (the Yukon uses BC curriculum with a few adaptations), but the programming, lesson delivery, increased First Nations–language instruction, and assessment methodology reflect the world views of the Yukon First Nations.[5]

The Tłı̨chǫ Land Claims and Self-Government Agreement—the first of its kind in the Northwest Territories—has had a great impact on the preservation and revitalization of Tłı̨chǫ language and culture. The Agreement established the Tłı̨chǫ Community Services Agency (TCSA) in 2005.[6] The TCSA manages the delivery of health services, social services, and education while also prioritizing and encouraging the usage of Tłı̨chǫ language throughout all levels of the community's government, schools, and other public services.

First Nations across Canada are participating in mineral exploration and mining operations through Impact and Benefit Agreements (contracts between bands and industry partners describing each partner's obligation for the business relationship), equity positions (where Indigenous groups get whole or part ownership of the project), and procurement agreements (contracting Indigenous businesses). The arrangements open the door for Nations to generate funds for language and culture revitalization and enhancement. Because of the confidential nature of Impact and Benefit Agreements (IBAs), few are publicly available. The First Nations LNG Alliance engaged in conversations with First Nations community leaders to develop a guide for First Nations in the design and implementation of IBAs. Community leaders highlighted to the Alliance "that IBAs ought to be directed towards securing the future of the community in ways that support the pursuit of self-determination through local procurement opportunities, business growth, educational improvements, housing, wages, the protection of lands, culture and language, and generally improving the quality of life in communities."[7] In some communities that have agreements with industrial developers, you'll see efforts to support culture, health, and well-being. These are all ways for communities to include their nation-building aspirations in everyday life.

A great example of this is the Raglan Agreement (1995), which was one of the first IBAs in Canada signed between a mining company (Raglan Mine) and Indigenous communities (the Makivik Corporation, the Inuit communities of Salluit and Kangiqsujuaq, and their respective landholding corporations).[8] Beyond the employment opportunities and profit-sharing provided by this IBA, Raglan Mine and the

Agreement also offer a number of programs that directly help local Inuit communities. The Raglan Education Fund "awards a minimum of $50,000 annually in scholarships to Nunavik students who pursue postsecondary, college or university education,"[9] and the Akkivik donations program has "contributed over $1.4 million to community initiatives" to date.[10] This IBA brings financial benefits to local Indigenous communities and gives Inuit youth the support to pursue higher education as well as job training and employment opportunities, allowing them to stay closer to home and their culture.

Following the 2015 *Truth and Reconciliation Commission of Canada: Calls to Action*, there has been some movement by the federal government to support Indigenous language revitalization. In 2019, the *Indigenous Languages Act* was passed. Section 6 of the Act states: "The Government of Canada recognizes that the rights of Indigenous peoples recognized and affirmed by section 35 of the *Constitution Act, 1982* include rights related to Indigenous languages."[11]

Recognition that Indigenous Rights include language rights is a major milestone in the work required to preserve Indigenous languages, as are the mechanisms within the *Indigenous Languages Act* to provide "adequate, sustainable and long-term funding for the reclamation, revitalization, maintenance and strengthening of Indigenous languages."[12] However, the Department of Canadian Heritage's Indigenous Languages Program, which is the primary source of funding for First Nations to develop language plans and support project-based language revitalization funding outside of schools, decreased First Nations languages funding by 56 per cent for 2024–25.[13]

Self-government agreements are opportunities for Nations to revitalize their languages, which are critical to preserving their history, customs, culture, protocols, and traditions with continued funding of these efforts.

{ 13 }

Socio-Economic Issues Can Be Remedied

EIGHT SOCIO-ECONOMIC issues of most significant concern for Indigenous Peoples in Canada are complex and intertwined. And the roots of each of these issues sit squarely in the *Indian Act* and colonialism.

Poorer Health

The World Health Organization's investigation into health determinants now recognizes European colonization as a common and fundamental underlying determinant of Indigenous health, resulting in Indigenous Peoples being at higher risk for illness and earlier death than non-Indigenous people.[1] In Canada, the physical, sexual, and psychological trauma experienced by survivors of the residential schools continues to impact the physical and mental health of survivors and generations of Indigenous families. Research into the long-lasting effects and how the intergenerational trauma is carried in the DNA of the survivors and passed down to their children is under way.[2]

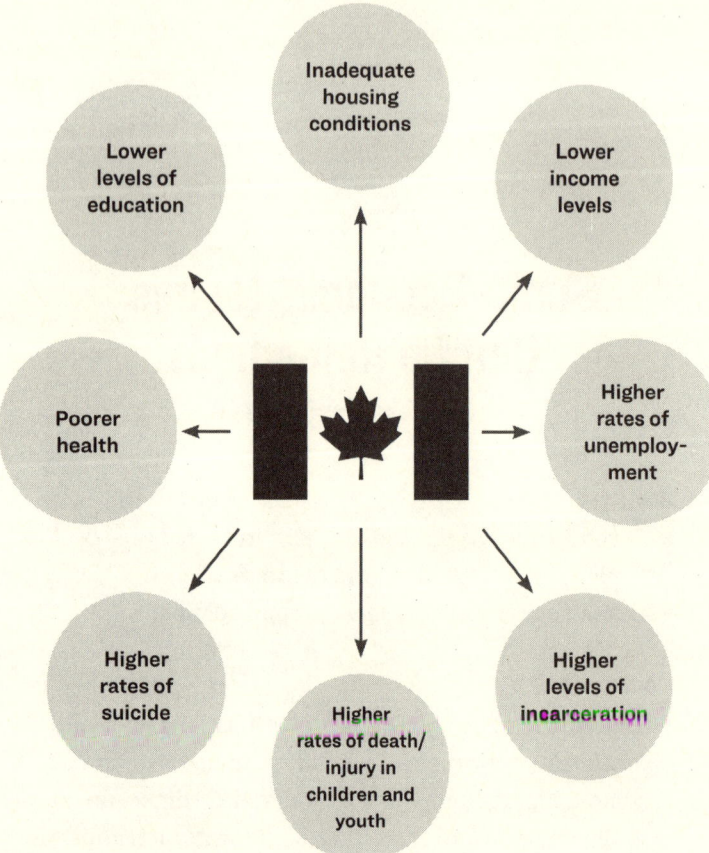

Lower Levels of Education

While Canada has one of the highest levels of educational attainment in the world, the rate of graduation for Indigenous students remains far lower than that of non-Indigenous students. For Indigenous students living on reserve, the gap is vast. According to a C.D. Howe

Institute study, only 48 per cent of young adults living on reserve have completed high school, while 75 per cent living off reserve have completed high school.[3]

Inadequate Housing Conditions

In 2021, almost one in six Indigenous Peoples (16.4 per cent) lived in a dwelling needing major repairs, a rate nearly three times higher than that of the non-Indigenous population (5.7 per cent). As well, 17.1 per cent of Indigenous Peoples lived in crowded housing—that is, housing not considered suitable for the number of people living there, according to the National Occupancy Standard.[4]

Lower Income Levels

According to the 2021 census, of the 1.8 million Indigenous Peoples in Canada, 18.8 per cent lived in a low-income household, as defined using the low-income measure after tax, compared with 10.7 per cent of the non-Indigenous population.[5]

Higher Rates of Unemployment

Indigenous Peoples have historically faced higher unemployment rates than non-Indigenous people.[6] The higher rate of unemployment is connected to lower levels of education, cultural differences, racism, discrimination/stereotypes, self-esteem, poverty, and poor housing, along with the lack of a driver's licence, access to transportation, and child care.[7]

Higher Levels of Incarceration

Despite Indigenous Peoples making up approximately 5 per cent of the total population in Canada, 32 per cent of federal inmates identify as Indigenous. Indigenous women now account for more than half of the female inmate population in Canadian prisons.[8]

Higher Rates of Death/Injury in Children and Youth

Accidents occur at disproportionately higher rates for Indigenous children and youth than for non-Indigenous youth.[9] And because of a shortage of health care resources in remote communities, injured Indigenous children on remote reserves are much less likely to receive rehabilitation or other support after being released from the hospital.

Higher Rates of Suicide

Indigenous Peoples in Canada have some of the highest rates of death by suicide in the world. Death by suicide and self-inflicted injuries are the leading causes of death for First Nations youth and adults up to 44 years of age.[10]

Indigenous Communities Address Socio-Economic Issues with Jurisdiction

Continuing to live as wards of the state under the *Indian Act* will only exacerbate these issues as the Indigenous population grows. Years of policy and strategy changes at the federal level have not fixed the issues. I believe it was Albert Einstein who said we cannot solve our problems with the same thinking we used to create them. To me, this statement sums up why the above issues continue to exist.

Communities themselves know their issues, needs, and priorities better than the federal government, so jurisdiction is better than programs, as it allows for communities to direct funding into programs that address the issues of most importance to them. Self-governance can provide the jurisdiction that Indigenous communities need to address these issues directly.

And there has been some progress already. For example, the Aboriginal Housing Management Association (AHMA) is an organization that works directly with the British Columbia government to provide housing and services to Indigenous Peoples living off reserve across the province. AHMA is the first "for Indigenous, by Indigenous" housing authority in Canada, and its services include advocacy, policy advancement, and financial support, to name just a few. Its website highlights that "AHMA members provide a spectrum of trauma-informed, culturally safe housing including affordable housing units, homeless shelters, transition homes, supportive housing, and assisted living facilities. Many of AHMA's members also offer support services including homelessness prevention, parenting skills, mental health programs, and substance use support, complex care, and more. In terms of scale, AHMA members make up over one-third of Indigenous housing providers in Canada."[11] The AHMA's multifaceted approach doesn't just address housing; it provides support for mental health, trauma, and substance abuse, and for multigenerational families.

Another example is the Yukon First Nation Education Directorate (YFNED), which was established in 2020 after the Chiefs Committee on Education called for change to the Yukon's public school system.[12] The YFNED's mission is to have "unified control over First Nation education so we can empower our people in our ways of knowing and prepare our children to be active participants in the current world." With this "unified control," the YFNED aims to improve the quality of education provided to First Nation students in the Yukon and emphasizes passing along cultural and traditional knowledge, values, language, and connection.[13]

I want to note, for clarity's sake, that the Yukon First Nation Education Directorate is different from the First Nation School Board (FNSB) that I mentioned in the previous chapter. The YFNED serves all Indigenous children up to age 18, while the FNSB specifically serves K-12 public school students. The YFNED delivers programs and services alongside schools, whereas the FNSB manages and operates the schools.[14] Regardless, both organizations demonstrate how giving control over education back to Indigenous communities allows them to improve their educational systems and pass on important Traditional Knowledge and languages to younger generations.

Lastly, I wanted to highlight the Nisga'a Nation's approach to justice, as seen in the *Nisga'a Final Agreement/Implementation Report 2021-2022*. The report details the Nation's policing services and its Access to Justice Department, which also includes various programs within Nisga'a communities that aim to address conflict resolution, crime prevention, support for crime victims, and alternative solutions for justice.[15] In particular, the Nation's Aboriginal Justice Program "encourages the revival of traditional Nisga'a ways of resolving conflict" and acts as the liaison "between Nisga'a communities and the Canadian justice system."[16] Returning justice to the hands of Indigenous local governments and the communities themselves is an effective way to prevent and police crime at the local level; to provide support for those affected by crime, violence, or injustice; and to revitalize traditional methods of resolution.

Self-governance, jurisdiction, and funding give Indigenous communities the ability to address and resolve the socio-economic issues that directly impact them most at the local level.

{ 14 }

The Infrastructure Gap Closes

PUBLIC INFRASTRUCTURE (roads, bridges, arenas, libraries, hospitals, schools, and so on) across Canada is aging and in poor condition. An example is the 2024 water main break in Calgary that had thousands of people managing their water for weeks.[1] There is an urgent need for significant long-term investments in infrastructure.

The investment required to bring the average First Nation's infrastructure on reserves to the average level of other communities is widely accepted to be at least $30 billion.[2]

Remote and northern communities often have the most challenging infrastructure issues. They're stuck in a vicious cycle. They lack the infrastructure required for economic development, which limits their ability to generate the necessary capital to create the infrastructure they need for economic development.

This excerpt from *Reducing the Barriers to Indigenous Economic Growth*, which was submitted to the House of Commons Standing Committee on Indigenous and Northern Affairs Canada in 2022, presents a clear picture of the infrastructure and economic development funding situation as of that year:

> The current government approach to funding is possibly the most significant challenge when it comes to infrastructure and economic development. [...]
>
> - Current annual capital funding available through ISC [Indigenous Services Canada] is around $2 billion. Decisions are made annually around how to allocate these monies. This compares to an identified and verifiable need for at least $30 billion.
>
> - Even prior to Covid-19, inflation on capital projects was higher than CPI [Consumer Price Index] inflation. As a result, unfunded needs are growing at a faster pace than ISC's annual investments. This means First Nations are falling further behind every year.
>
> - Projects are often funded based on dollars available, rather than need, urgency, or potential impact.
>
> - Communities stand in-line each year, and if not selected then stand in the same line next year. The gap continues to grow.
>
> - Funding provided is generally for initial construction, without any allocation available for ongoing operations and maintenance. Infrastructure in First

Nations often does not meet the expected lifespan. As well, no monitoring of the annual maintenance occurs.[3]

In 2021, the federal government announced the National Infrastructure Assessment[4] to measure Canada's infrastructure needs and establish a long-term vision, to improve coordination among infrastructure owners and funders, and to determine the best ways to fund and finance infrastructure. Submissions to the ensuing report, *Building Pathways to 2050: Moving Forward on the National Infrastructure Assessment*, emphasized "the importance of supporting capacity-building (e.g., supporting asset management initiatives) and of recognizing Indigenous leadership by investing in the agency of Indigenous peoples and communities, supporting Indigenous-led and delivered solutions, equipping Indigenous peoples with equitable resources, and ensuring appropriate access to funding."[5]

The report notes "an emphasis on key infrastructure issues [in Indigenous communities], including diesel dependency, the need for investments in safe and efficient transportation and trade corridors, high-speed broadband connectivity and workforce and skills training. Access to affordable capital for investments in major projects as equity partners and access to adequate early-stage project capacity and development funding were raised as key issues."[6]

Indigenous Nations are in the best position to understand the needs of their communities and to provide more unified decisions, made faster and based on the community's needs and values. With consistent funding being critical to investing in infrastructure—such as roads, water, sewer systems, community parks, fire safety, cultural centres, museums, and cultural gathering places such as longhouses, big houses, or dance grounds—self-government agreements are one way to meet the funding needs. Parts XX and XXI of the Westbank First Nation Self-Government Agreement provides the Westbank First Nation with jurisdiction over infrastructure, while the Anishinabek Nation Governance Agreement and the Tla'amin Final Agreement (2014)[7] have recognized infrastructure as an area for future control by self-governing communities.

DRINKING WATER ADVISORIES

Of all the on-reserve infrastructure issues, the lack of clean water perhaps resonates with us all. Regularly turning on the tap for a glass of water is a natural action for most Canadians, but not so much for many Indigenous Peoples on reserve.

At any given time, new drinking water advisories in First Nations communities are issued and existing advisories are revoked.[8] Some of the advisories are short term, while some communities have endured long-term drinking water advisories for decades.[9]

Thousands of Indigenous Peoples have grown up never knowing what it's like to turn on the tap and pour a glass of clean water. In some communities, entire generations have grown up under various degrees of drinking water advisories.[10] The Neskantaga First Nation in northern Ontario, with a population of about 300,[11] has had a drinking water advisory in place since 1996.[12] That means one whole generation has grown up under a drinking water advisory, and now a second generation is growing up having never turned on the tap for a glass of water.

In 2010, the United Nations declared water and sanitation as human rights, acknowledging they are essential to the realization of all other rights.[13]

{ 15 }

Self-Reliance and Economic Reconciliation Can Begin with Small Actions

ECONOMIC RECONCILIATION is essential if Canada is going to close the socio-economic gaps between Indigenous and non-Indigenous people in Canada.

Article 21.1 of the UN Declaration on the Rights of Indigenous Peoples states: "Indigenous peoples have the right, without discrimination, to the improvement of their economic and social conditions, including, inter alia, in the areas of education, employment, vocational training and retraining, housing, sanitation, health and social security."[1]

Indigenous Nations want to participate in the economic mainstream without relying on federal funding to meet their community needs. They want to develop own-source revenue opportunities and participate in a way that lets them protect and nurture their cultures.

A significant barrier to economic reconciliation is section 89 of the *Indian Act*, which reads: "Subject to this Act, the real and personal property of an Indian or a band situated on a reserve is not subject to charge, pledge, mortgage, attachment, levy, seizure, distress or execution in favour or at the instance of any person other than an Indian or a band."[2]

The rationale behind section 89 was to protect the reserve land base and personal property of Indians and Indian bands. But this "protection" restricts access to secured loans, because lending institutions cannot seize collateral on reserves. Not being able to secure loans poses a significant barrier for Nations to realize Indigenous self-reliance.

Get Behind the Wheel, *Indian Act* Style

To share an example of how the reserve system and the *Indian Act* can limit a person's prospects, I'll take you back to my college days, when I was enrolled in business administration and taking a business credit course. In that course, we learned what a person needed to have good credit, how to keep it, and how to analyze whether you met the credit criteria.

Good credit boiled down to having a postsecondary education, a steady employer, and positive future prospects you could demonstrate. Following college, I got married and had a great job at BC Hydro. Life was looking pretty darn good, even from a credit perspective. Eventually I needed a new vehicle, so I went to the local car dealer and arranged a purchase with the salesperson, who referred me to the business agent for the loan and car transfer paperwork. As we completed the paperwork, she ran me through a "soft" interview process. One of the questions was about my Indian status. As soon as I affirmed that I was a Status Indian, she asked if the car would be delivered to the reserve so the transactional taxes could be exempted from the purchase price. The next question she asked me was, "Do you have someone who can co-sign for you?"

I realized that because I was a Status Indian, they were worried that if I drove the car away to the reserve and decided not to pay for it, they wouldn't be able to seize it, as reserves are not subject to seizure under legal process. I was surprised and a little upset that I could not get credit on my own. I met all the criteria discussed in my business credit course, but I would have to ask my wife, who is not Indigenous, to co-sign for me if I wanted to buy a vehicle. It certainly was a good lesson in some of the restrictions of the *Indian Act* and a major reason for us to get beyond it. These kinds of restrictions imposed by the *Indian Act* means that Indigenous Peoples will never be able to fully participate in the economy and access capital—nobody wants to lend you money if they can't repossess what you're borrowing against. In other words, the *Indian Act* is continuing to do exactly what it was not designed to do: isolate Indigenous Peoples from mainstream society, instead of assimilate.

Taxation Options for First Nations

For small, remote communities with limited infrastructure, the challenge of developing their own revenue sources is particularly acute. They may have fly-in access only or depend on ice roads for part of the year. They also may not have reliable internet service. Building a business without the necessities many of us take for granted is pretty hard.

In a 2023 statement, Chief Commissioner of the First Nations Tax Commission C.T. (Manny) Jules outlined: "Between 1867 and 1930, First Nations were systematically legislated out of the Canadian federation and economy. All First Nation government powers, including the ability to raise revenues to finance those powers, were removed and distributed between the federal and provincial governments. This has caused ongoing First Nation dependency, poverty, and service quality disparity."[3]

There are, however, some avenues for own-source revenue that nations can engage with.

Personal Taxation

The *First Nations Goods and Services Tax Act* allows Indigenous governing bodies to pass laws imposing a goods and services tax on all its residents, including Status Indians.[4] This can be an effective way for a Nation to capture revenues arising from economic activity on their traditional lands or reserves.

Income tax is another source of revenues for Indigenous governing bodies, which we covered in chapter 11, "Tax Is Included," in relation to how self-government agreements are removing *Indian Act* tax exemptions and allowing Nations to generate their own revenue for programs, services, and investments.

Real Property Taxation on Treaty and Traditional Territory

Similar to taxation used by other governments in Canada, property taxes are an annual tax based on the value of real property such as land, buildings, transmission lines, towers, and so on. Recall from chapter 11 that the Tsawwassen First Nation's projects will be generating almost $33 million in revenue per year, mainly through taxes and lease revenue. The 2023–24 annual report for the Westbank First Nation shows property tax revenue at over $19 million.[5]

Resource Revenue Sharing

Resource revenue sharing is "receiving a share of the fiscal benefits from the use of ancestral land and the resources on it."[6] This is not a new idea for Nations. Since 2012, the First Nations Tax Commission has been calling for a First Nations Resource Charge to capture revenue from the resources on their traditional lands. This is seen as Nations having fiscal jurisdiction over resource projects on their lands.

A current example of resource revenue sharing is the Nisga'a Nation collecting forestry stumpage fees—fees that are paid to the Nisga'a Nation from timber collected from Nisga'a lands.[7] But this is not quite the same as the proposed First Nations Resource Charge.

The difference between the Nisga'a arrangement and the First Nations Resource Charge is that the latter would "provide First Nations the option to implement a pre-specified charge regime based on land use and resources in their territory or ancestral lands. The charge system would be established in First Nation law. There will be distinct charges for each resource project type, which would be standardized throughout a province or possibly the country. For example, there would be distinct charge rates and bases for mining, pipelines, forestry and other eligible projects."[8] This would create economic certainty for resource companies and a steady revenue stream for Nations.

I have always told our learners that First Nations are not against development, but it can't be development at all costs. First Nations want to be involved in the decision-making process and to approve those developments, and they should benefit from them when they are on reserve and traditional lands.

Resource revenue sharing could be a game-changer for First Nations and their pursuit of self-governance and self-reliance. Formally involving First Nations in development would also reduce some of the friction from the past. Having legislation in place to guide this process would provide all Nations with a more diversified economy.

Impact and Benefit Agreements

An Impact and Benefit Agreement (IBA) is an agreement between a First Nation and a project proponent in a First Nation's Traditional or Treaty Territory. In chapter 12, we talked about how IBAs can support language rights. They can also include business and procurement opportunities; employment; education and training; and environmental, archaeological, and Traditional Knowledge protection.

Take Voisey's Bay Mine in Labrador, for instance. After mining company Vale Canada Ltd. (formerly, Vale Inco) purchased Voisey's Bay nickel, copper, and cobalt deposits, the company was met with initial pushback by the

Labrador Inuit Association (LIA) and the Innu Nation. In 2002, after some negotiation and consultation, both the LIA and Innu Nation signed IBAs with Vale Inco.[9] These IBAs in Voisey's Bay have resulted in preferential employment for Inuit and Innu people and the establishment of the Labrador Aboriginal Training Partnership, which recruits and trains Indigenous workers, allowing them to gain skills and job experience.[10] Additionally, these IBAs called for the Innu to create a full-time environmental monitor at the mine, which has since expanded into four monitors at the Voisey's Bay site, and the establishment of a similar Inuit program called the Nunatsiavut Guardians. Their job is to ensure the protection of the land and local wildlife, and monitor any potential environmental hazards.[11] These IBAs are an excellent example of how Indigenous consultation and cooperation can lead to employment and training opportunities, as well as environmental and Traditional Knowledge protections.

Equity Positions

One example of an equity position is direct equity ownership in major projects. This is next-level from resource revenue sharing and IBA arrangements. Funding for Indigenous equity projects comes from various sources, including government grants, the Canada Infrastructure Bank, and private lending. An equity position could include a nation's citizens having equal shares in a business owned by the community.

Increasingly, large companies are incorporating equity positions in new projects. For example, in 2024, BC Hydro announced nine projects that required a minimum of

25 per cent equity ownership by First Nations; in fact, eight out of the nine projects will have at least 51 per cent equity ownership.[12] Partnering with Indigenous Peoples and incorporating direct equity ownership in projects is mutually beneficial. Much like IBAs, direct equity positions recognize and utilize Indigenous knowledge of Traditional Territories, ensure more effective consultation with Indigenous communities, and can include environmental protections, while also demonstrating an important step towards Indigenous economic reconciliation.

Gaming

Bill S-268 (*An Act to Amend the Criminal Code and the Indian Act*), in its second reading at the time of writing, seeks to amend Canada's *Criminal Code* to provide the governing body of a First Nation with "exclusive authority to conduct and manage a lottery scheme on its reserve and to license the conduct and management of a lottery scheme by other persons and entities on its reserve."[13] Bill S-268 opens up possibilities of tremendous revenue and financial gains for First Nations.

Economic Independence

All Canadians will benefit when Indigenous Nations realize economic sustainability because they will contribute to local, regional, and national economies. And we have an opportunity to support where we can. The Truth and Reconciliation Commission's 92nd Call to Action is as follows:

Business and Reconciliation

92. We call upon the corporate sector in Canada to adopt the United Nations Declaration on the Rights of Indigenous Peoples as a reconciliation framework and to apply its principles, norms, and standards to corporate policy and core operational activities involving Indigenous Peoples and their lands and resources. This would include, but not be limited to, the following:

i. Commit to meaningful consultation, building respectful relationships, and obtaining the Free, Prior, and Informed Consent of Indigenous Peoples before proceeding with economic development projects.

ii. Ensure that Aboriginal peoples have equitable access to jobs, training, and education opportunities in the corporate sector, and that Aboriginal communities gain long-term sustainable benefits from economic development projects.

iii. Provide education for management and staff on the history of Aboriginal peoples, including the history and legacy of residential schools, the United Nations Declaration on the Rights of Indigenous Peoples, Treaties and Aboriginal rights, Indigenous law, and Aboriginal-Crown relations. This will require skills based training in intercultural competency, conflict resolution, human rights, and anti-racism.[14]

Consider this: A $70,000 personal annual income brings in expenditure funds, which, if you were to multiply by 10 or 100 or 1,000 jobs, could change a community completely. I've talked to many Indigenous leaders who have commented that just simple things like employment can change the outcome for individuals, communities, and Nations.

Small steps add up. Economic independence does not have to be gained through expansive government programs. It can begin with a small action such as offering training and employment, securing procurement, engaging Indigenous businesses to help with your business or your government, or even organizing bingo nights (see the sidebar "The Seminal Seminole Example"). Taking those small steps can put us into a different place as we look forward to the future for all our kids.

THE SEMINAL SEMINOLE EXAMPLE

"I don't think the measure of how much money comes into the tribe is the benchmark," said former Seminole Tribe Vice-Chair Max Osceola Jr. "I think the measurement is what you do with it. Money only buys convenience. It doesn't buy character."[15]

For years I've been fascinated by the Seminole Tribe's purchase of the Hard Rock International franchise of hotels, restaurants, and related businesses. While visiting their Ah-Tah-Thi-Ki Museum in Florida, I received a tour of the facilities with the manager. My first question was, "How did a small tribe raise the funds to purchase a major franchise?"

The answer is inspirational. The Tribal Council realized that they were not going to survive as a people if they waited for the US federal Bureau of Indian Affairs to save them and their culture and lift them out of poverty. They needed their own sources of funding. So they held a bingo night, which was so successful that they held another and another. In 1979, they had the funds to buy a bingo hall in Tampa, FL, becoming the first tribe in the US to offer high-stakes gambling.

In 2007, the Seminoles became the first American Indian tribe to buy a global brand, purchasing Hard Rock International from UK-based The Rank Group PLC for $965 million. The tribe also operates a string of casinos in Florida and owns the chain of Hard Rock hotels and casinos with locations in 76 countries. In 2024, it added The Mirage in Las Vegas to its string of operations. As the Seminole Tribe website states:

> Today, most Tribal members are afforded modern housing and health care. The Seminole Tribe spends over $1 million each year on education alone, including grants-in-aid to promising Tribal college students and the operation of the Ahfachkee Indian School. Over 300 Tribal members are employed by the Seminole Tribe in dozens of governmental departments, including legal and law enforcement staffs. Dozens of new enterprises, operated by Tribal members, are supported by both the Tribal Council and Board. [...] Seminole Tribe of Florida is exempt from all federal or state taxes, although individual Tribal members are liable for the same state and federal taxes as any citizen.[16]

It all began with an idea and a decision, and it was made possible by a bingo game.

I share this story to illustrate what can be accomplished by first admitting the issue—the Seminoles realized they weren't going to survive as a people with the type of help on offer from the government. Second, they decided to take action and get into the economy. Third, they acted with the smallest of ideas and kept moving forward by raising funds to change the outcome and narrative of their reality.

{ 16 }

Free, Prior, and Informed Consent Must Be Obtained

ARTICLE 32.2 of the UN Declaration on the Rights of Indigenous Peoples reads: "States shall consult and cooperate in good faith with the indigenous peoples concerned through their own representative institutions in order to obtain their free and informed consent prior to the approval of any project affecting their lands or territories and other resources, particularly in connection with the development, utilization or exploitation of mineral, water or other resources."[1]

In Canada, the resource extractive sector derives much of its materials from the lands and waters of Traditional and Treaty Lands of Indigenous Peoples. The presence and effects of these industries frequently impact Indigenous lands and resources. Through this lens, if the *UN Declaration on the Rights of Indigenous Peoples Act* is to be honoured, understanding the right to Free, Prior, and Informed Consent is essential.

Here's a simple explainer of what Free, Prior, and Informed Consent looks like: The decision-making process must be free of pressure or coercion. Peoples, Nations, or communities must be given ample time to gather and, if necessary, translate information prior to being asked to make a decision. Consultation or discussions leading up to consent must be held within a time frame that allows that particular people, Nation, or community ample time for information-gathering and consultation within the community for an informed decision to be made. Consent to an agreement for a project to proceed must be reached via a decision-making process or structure that is consistent with that particular people, Nation, or community.

The big question that's often asked is, "Who do we talk to?" For a very long time, the rule of thumb was that, when it came to development, you were to talk to the Elected Band Chief and Council, as it was assumed that they were the legitimate and legal government. In reality, they were not necessarily as legitimate and legal as initially considered. They are imposed governments, so consultation with them in the context of the UN Declaration and obtaining Free, Prior, and Informed Consent is incorrect because "free" means you are supposed to be able to talk to all Nation members about projects, not necessarily the Band Chief and Council alone.

Can the Government of Canada create and fund a political entity—a Band Chief and Council—and then go to it for decisions on projects the Government of Canada wants to see built? In the context of the UN Declaration and Free, Prior, and Informed Consent, ethically, no, it can't, because it created the Band Chief and Council positions, and the people in those roles are not without conflict of interest, because the federal government pays their salaries and funds their programs.

Free, Prior, and Informed Consent and the Duty to Consult

All levels of government want to generate funds to provide programs and services to Canadians through resource development. However, the legal requirements of the duty to consult on Indigenous issues, environmental matters, and other matters is frequently seen as red tape that gets in the way. If governments, which have the duty to consult, sometimes delegate the administrative and procedural aspects to industrial developers who don't do adequate and meaningful consultation, we run into problems with project delays because of the resulting legal challenges to the consultation process, through a judicial review mechanism. There have been hundreds of cases where Indigenous Peoples have challenged the Crown's adequacy and meaningfulness of consultation, creating economic uncertainty and risk for companies and the economy.

In December 1997, the *Delgamuukw v. British Columbia* ruling came out. This ruling confirmed that Aboriginal Title exists in British Columbia—a right to the land itself (not simply the right to fish, hunt, and gather on the land), and that, according to the BC Treaty Commission, "when dealing with Crown land, the government must consult with and may have to compensate First Nations whose rights are affected."[2]

At the time, high-ranking government lawyers told me that they were instructed to test the law. They first focused their energies on determining if there were cases where there was no duty to consult. As it became clear from Supreme Court judges that there is always a duty to consult, government lawyers shifted their focus to clarifying what was considered legally adequate and meaningful consultation. This focus can be described as looking for the boundaries. More than 150 cases have wrestled with the question alone of adequacy and meaningfulness of consultation.

A BRIEF HISTORY OF DELGAMUUKW AND GISDAY'WAY

Three cases collectively called "Delgamuukw" are a critical part of the constitutional puzzle of Aboriginal rights and title for British Columbia and all of Canada. In my opinion, "Delgamuukw and Gisday'way" is a better and more accurate way to refer to these cases, as "Delgamuukw" and "Gisday'way" are the names of the Hereditary Chiefs of the Gitxsan and Wet'suwet'en who brought the cases forward. Notice I did not say "Band Chiefs." This case is an example of the "free" in Free, Prior, and Informed Consent.

In 1984, 35 Gitxsan and 13 Wet'suwet'en Hereditary Chiefs asked the Supreme Court of British Columbia to recognize their ownership of 57,000 square kilometres of land in northwestern BC, to confirm their right to govern their Traditional Territories, and to award compensation for loss of their lands and resources. The Gitxsan and Wet'suwet'en decided to proceed with trial by judge alone (rather than by judge and jury) and submitted an enormous body of oral and written evidence (the court transcript covered 369 days of proceedings) regarding the nature and duration of their use and occupation of their traditional lands.

In his reasons for judgment released in 1991, Chief Justice Allan McEachern, at trial in the lower court, left open the possibility that Aboriginal Rights may arise through the use and occupation of specific lands for Aboriginal purposes for an indefinite (and lengthy) period prior to British sovereignty. However, he ruled that in any event, the Crown had extinguished any such Aboriginal Rights by its imposition of complete dominion over the colonial territory prior to BC joining Confederation in 1871.[3] The Gitxsan and Wet'suwet'en appealed.

In 1993, the BC Court of Appeal reversed much of the lower court's decision and ruled instead that the Gitxsan and Wet'suwet'en peoples do have "unextinguished non-exclusive Aboriginal rights, other than a right of ownership," to much of their Traditional Territory. In addition, the appeal court justices strongly recommended that the scope and content of those rights would best be defined through negotiation rather than litigation. The British Columbia government appealed to the Supreme Court of Canada.[4]

On December 11, 1997, a unanimous Supreme Court of Canada judgment provided a vital definition and description of Aboriginal Title, affirming the legal validity of Aboriginal oral history and clarifying the nature of the Crown's duties of consultation and accommodation in the context of Aboriginal Rights infringement.[5] The *Delgamuukw* decision is, simply put, the reason we all do Indigenous consultation on everything that gets built or developed.

Coastal GasLink and Free, Prior, and Informed Consent

Despite the 1997 *Delgamuukw* ruling, governments and corporations are still struggling to attain Free, Prior, and Informed Consent. A recent example comes in the form of the Coastal GasLink project. In the early 2020s, after the Province of British Columbia issued permits, Coastal GasLink began construction of a pipeline on traditional, unceded Wet'suwet'en lands—without Free, Prior, and Informed Consent of the Hereditary Chiefs. The company did enter into an Impact and Benefit Agreement with Elected Chiefs, but there are all kinds of problems with talking to just the Elected Chiefs and Councils. The approach should have included, at the very least, the Band Chiefs, the Hereditary Chiefs, as well as the membership of the Indigenous community—because an often-overlooked but vital factor is that the rights of Indigenous Peoples are collectively held. Ignoring the Hereditary Chiefs and the community created a situation that resulted in acrimony, legal challenges, blockades, negative media campaigns, and economic uncertainty. It also caused deep divisions within communities and family members in those communities, and harmed relations between the communities and local municipalities.

Had the principles of Free, Prior, and Informed Consent been followed, it would have helped us, as a country, prevent the big problems that erupted over the Coastal GasLink project. Seeking signed agreements with just the Elected Chiefs and Councils all along the pipeline corridor and ignoring the Hereditary Chiefs put the project, its proponents, the land defenders, Indigenous relations in general, and the Canadian economy in peril.[6] By ignoring the Hereditary Chiefs, the project veered into an unworkable situation that would move forward only with years of legal manoeuvring and lengthy project delays.

Failing to recognize and affirm Indigenous Rights and Title is why big resource projects sometimes get into trouble. When an Indigenous community raises an issue they have with a project, and the government and project proponents do not talk about the issue with them, project approval may be delayed. Think back to another example: The Trans Mountain Pipeline expansion project aimed to increase the capacity of pipelines running from Edmonton, AB, all the way to Burnaby, BC.[7] Indigenous Nations, and others, were concerned about the impacts of the increase in tanker traffic on the southern resident orcas in BC. The scope of consideration of the effects of the pipeline of the Canada Energy Regulator (formerly, the National Energy Board) was largely limited to impacts on land. Increased tanker traffic in waters home to the southern resident orcas, an issue raised by Indigenous Nations during the consultation process, was considered to be beyond the scope of the National Energy Board's mandate. This left the issue, which would have been the basis for a judicial review, unresolved. When the Federal Court of Appeal quashed approvals for the Trans Mountain Pipeline expansion, the findings included the inadequacies of the consultation process on the part of Canada, which owed a duty of adequate and meaningful consultation to each Indigenous community affected and a duty of deep consultation to each Indigenous applicant. It is very difficult to recognize and affirm the rights of Nations when you are not even willing or able to talk to them about their concerns. Such was the case in ignoring the resident orcas.

To have conversations with Indigenous leadership, knowing that they are free from outside influence and coercion, we need to support communities that want to move away from the system imposed by the *Indian Act* and towards Indigenous self-government. As we saw with Coastal GasLink focusing their consultations with Band Chiefs and Councils, the impacts of not obtaining the free consent of members of all affected Nations led to significant cost overruns and delays. Self-government agreements can provide a clearer path to the Nation's preferred leadership for business and governments, thus clarifying who is to be consulted on such projects.

{ 17 }

Territories Can Overlap

~~~~~~~~~~

For millennia, Indigenous Peoples managed their relationships through protocols and laws that respected each other's sovereignty, lands, and resources. These relationships were disrupted through colonization and the imposition of the *Indian Act* and all that it brought to their lives—the reserve system, the introduction of the Elected Band Chief and Council system of governance, expropriation of lands, and violation of historic treaties.

This disruption led to Canadian government–enforced overlapping territories, which caused issues not only in the settlement of land claims but also in terms of self-government agreements. Who has jurisdiction? Who has access to resources? Whose cultural laws apply? These are difficult questions to answer when two or more communities claim the same piece of territory.

The overlapping territory problem is exacerbated by the treaty commission process, which requires that overlaps be worked out among the communities involved before proceeding deeper into the process.[1] But in some cases, the government has further exacerbated the situation by proceeding with treaty negotiations even with outstanding overlapping territory issues.[2]

I would also like to add that historically, overlapping territories arose for strategic purposes, such as intermarriage for shared access to resources. This is considered a customary element of overlapping territory.

Whatever the case, overlapping territories for custom and legal reasons will continue to exist and occur as we continue our journey to dismantling the *Indian Act*.

{ 18 }

Self-Administration Is Not Self-Government

THE GOAL of the *Indian Act* over history can be summarized by this statement from Duncan Campbell Scott, Deputy Superintendent of the Department of Indian Affairs (1913–32): "I want to get rid of the Indian problem. Our objective is to continue until there is not a single Indian in Canada that has not been absorbed into the body politic and there is no Indian question, and no Indian Department."[1]

What began in 1876 continues today, albeit in a markedly different format. With the current mandate to "support and empower Indigenous peoples to independently deliver services and address the socio-economic conditions in their communities,"[2] Indigenous Services Canada delegates the delivery of some services to First Nations governments and organizations under the auspices of "support and empowerment."

This divestment, or downloading, of responsibility onto the shoulders of band administrators looks like this, in the words of Julie Williams, former Inherent Rights Fellow at the Centre for First Nations Governance and researcher at the Rebuilding First Nations Governance Program at Carleton University:

> First Nations take on the duties to deliver services like education, create by-laws and undertake certain financial administration, but are constrained by the laws and policies set by Canada and the provinces. For example, under the *Indian Act*, First Nations children on reserve go to schools that are run by their band, but they must learn the provincial or territorial curriculum. The spending of funds to deliver programs must adhere to federal rules and are accompanied by extensive reporting requirements where the First Nation's primary accountability is to Canada through the Minister of Indigenous Services Canada, not to their citizens.[3]

Administering programs and service delivery controlled by an outside agency is neither empowerment nor self-government. It is a step down the path to Scott's goal of "no Indian Department," which, when coupled with the ever-narrowing status criteria, gets rid of "the Indian problem."

As we move forward with dismantling the *Indian Act*, the process will be more community-driven, and I would like to think that the process of applying for citizenship will yield a positive user experience.

"Everything about us by us."

{ 19 }

Supporting Self-Government Is an Economic and Moral Opportunity

As DISCUSSED early in this book, King George III's Royal Proclamation of 1763 states: "It is just and reasonable, and essential to Our Interest and the Security of Our Colonies, that the several Nations or Tribes of Indians with whom We are connected, and who live under Our Protection, should not be molested or disturbed in the Possession of such Parts of Our Dominions and Territories as, not having been ceded to, or purchased by Us, are reserved to them, or any of them, as their Hunting Grounds."[1]

The Proclamation was a strategic move by the king to secure military and economic alliances at a time when other competing crowns were vying for control of what we now call Canada. The Proclamation was a moral stance and a business case for the king. Self-government aligns with the aspirational goal of King George III's Royal Proclamation.

The federal government spends billions on programs and services every year as part of its fiduciary duty towards "Indians, and Lands reserved for the Indians." The results remain relatively dismal despite the vast amounts of money poured into programs and services. Federal government documentation states: "Spending on Indigenous priorities has increased significantly since 2015 (181 per cent) with spending for 2023–24 estimated to be over $30.5 billion, rising further to a forecast of approximately $32 billion in 2024–25. Notably, Budget 2024 includes $2.3 billion over five years to renew existing programming."[2]

But as Anishinaabe educator Hayden King and Anishinaabe scholar Riley Yesno point out: "Of the 47 funding items for Indigenous initiatives, only 9.8% (946.6 million) went directly to Indigenous organizations, service providers and communities. The majority of the funding went to government departments and external organizations and agencies."[3]

It's time to really consider how Canada invests in its relationships with Indigenous Peoples, particularly Status Indians. I would argue that it makes good business sense to get away from this scenario, as it leads to lots of issues, as we have seen throughout this book, and to instead find ways to support self-reliance. "A hand up, as opposed to a handout," as former Chief Councillor Gibby Jacob of the Squamish Nation once said to me.

The Country Needs Economic Certainty

Economic certainty in Canada means no need for Indigenous protests, blockades, negative media campaigns, and legal challenges when it comes to industrial or infrastructure development because Indigenous Peoples are participating in decision-making and outcomes. Canada, at its financial core, is an industrial development country. We rely heavily on natural resource extraction activities such as forestry, mining, oil and gas, and other commodities to drive our economy forward and to make us a wealthy and prosperous nation. Some of the large oil-and-gas projects in recent history have struggled to be built in a timely fashion because of protests by Indigenous Peoples who were willing to challenge them legally.

Think of the Coastal GasLink pipeline project and how consultation was handled with the Wet'suwet'en First Nation Hereditary Chiefs, which was discussed in chapter 16, "Free, Prior, and Informed Consent Must Be Obtained." If the government and project proponents had worked closely with the Hereditary Chiefs and community members all along the pipeline as they did with the Elected Band Chiefs, we possibly could have avoided much of the economic impacts of the railroad shutdown, protests across the country, confrontations with enforcement agencies, and negative media campaigns. The blockades and the government's response drew international media attention in addition to billions in economic impacts.[4]

An overall sense of economic uncertainty prevails while governments and businesses struggle to push through these big projects without adequate and meaningful consultation, relying on governance determined by the *Indian Act*.

The Human Rights Case

Canada has always been seen as a great place to live, where people can pursue the Canadian dream and enjoy the freedom and prosperity that this country offers. However, that the people who have been here from time immemorial have been frozen out of those aspirations is a mismatch. Dismantling the *Indian Act* can help us fix this situation by giving Indigenous Peoples an opportunity to participate in the economic mainstream. It can promote social integration, ensure equal rights and opportunities for all Canadians, and strengthen the social fabric of our country. We can live up to our constitutional commitments to Indigenous Peoples and ensure everyone can live the Canadian dream.

Let's address a pressing issue. The *Indian Act*, in its current form, contradicts Canada's human rights legislation. It is an anti-human rights instrument. The purpose of the *Canadian Human Rights Act* is set out in section 2, which states "that all individuals should have an opportunity equal with other individuals to make for themselves the lives that they are able and wish to have and to have their needs accommodated, consistent with their duties and obligations as members of society, without being hindered in or prevented from doing so by discriminatory practices based on race, [etc.]."[5] The *Indian Act* does just the opposite.

Canada is seen as a champion for human rights issues around the world, and Canadians are well regarded globally for their humanitarian work. It is hard to reconcile the disparity between people living on reserves—often referred to as "third-world communities"—and what is happening in the rest of Canada.

It would be hard for Status Indians living on reserve to catch up or get ahead while living with the restrictions of the *Indian Act*, such as not owning the houses they live in or the land they live on, which is not subject to seizure under legal process. All of this keeps "Indians, and Lands reserved for the Indians" separate from the rest of the population.

King George III originally envisioned a relationship based on military and economic alliances, which was beneficial for all parties. However, the *Indian Act* replaced this system, leading to declining economic alliances and increased and inefficient resource allocation to *Indian Act* programs. To move forward, the focus should shift away from programs, protests, and legal battles, reducing economic uncertainty and creating more economic opportunities. Addressing human rights issues, such as the *Indian Act* restrictions, will further benefit Indigenous communities and all Canadians. It will also match our human rights objectives with our actions and improve our overall image as a country.

{ 20 }

Local Governments Can Support Self-Government

LOCAL GOVERNMENTS have more direct relationships with Indigenous communities, based on proximity and mutual interests, than their provincial or federal counterparts, who have constitutional and legal obligations to Indigenous Peoples. There is an abundance of opportunities for local governments to build supportive relationships with their Indigenous neighbours to prepare for future self-government. Here are a few suggestions:

- Develop an action plan for the Truth and Reconciliation Calls to Action. Begin with number 43: "We call upon federal, provincial, territorial, and municipal governments to fully adopt and implement the United Nations Declaration on the Rights of Indigenous Peoples as the framework for reconciliation."[1]

- Co-develop a framework agreement for government-to-government relations. One example that could be adapted and built upon is the memorandum of understanding (MOU) between the W̱SÁNEĆ Leadership Council Society and the District of Saanich. This MOU includes sections on environmental concerns, recognition of the United Nations Declaration on the Rights of Indigenous Peoples, and parks management, to name a few.[2] The objective is to co-develop management plans for the District of Saanich and the W̱SÁNEĆ Leadership Council.

- Provide training for all staff and volunteers to build a foundational understanding of the rights of Indigenous Peoples; the UN Declaration; Indigenous history; treaties; Indigenous-specific racism; the dynamics of respectful, effective, and sustainable relations; and meaningful reconciliation. Preferably from Indigenous-led businesses and trainers.

- Invite Indigenous neighbours to guide events for National Indigenous Peoples Day (June 21) and the National Day for Truth and Reconciliation (September 30).

- Publicly recognize the history of the Indigenous Peoples in the region.

- Establish an Indigenous Storyteller-in-Residence program at the public library.

- Offer lessons in the languages of the Indigenous Peoples in the region.

- Display art from local Indigenous communities in public buildings.

- Invite Indigenous Peoples to guide the development of culturally safe emergency planning.
- Work together with Indigenous communities on direct funding opportunities.
- Establish resource management partnerships with Indigenous communities.
- Involve Indigenous communities in local government land use planning where interests overlap or align.
- Jointly pursue economic development with Indigenous communities.
- Share tourism or agricultural ventures with Indigenous communities.

Looking to the friendship agreement between the Haisla Nation Council and the District of Kitimat in British Columbia,[3] local governments across the country can develop friendship agreements that could include the following principles:

- respect and recognition
- collaboration and partnership
- inclusivity and diversity
- transparency and accountability
- sustainability
- cultural preservation and awareness
- empowerment and capacity-building

As well, local governments can collaborate with Indigenous communities on initiatives to address issues that are important to both parties:

- mental health
- the opioid epidemic
- homelessness
- poverty
- the safety of women and girls
- youth
- climate change threats

VICTORIA'S RECONCILIATION CONTRIBUTION FUND

This initiative in Victoria caught my attention. It's such a simple action.

In 2022, the City of Victoria established the Reconciliation Contribution Fund.[4] Contributions aim to recognize that the wealth generated by the municipality and its residents comes from the lands and waters of the lək̓ʷəŋən (Lekwungen) people. This wealth includes property ownership and associated taxes.

Property tax notices include information about the Reconciliation Contribution Fund. Victoria property owners are encouraged to contribute an additional amount equal to 5 or 10 per cent of their property taxes or another amount they choose.

This voluntary contribution is separate from the annual property tax payment. The total value of each voluntary contribution goes directly to the Xwsepsum and Songhees nations.

{ 21 }

Self-Government Is Achievable

I WAS MOTIVATED by a specific topic when I first started writing this book. Many of you who read the original *21 Things You May Not Know About the Indian Act* or attended one of the hundreds of presentations related to it—either at your workplace or in one of my numerous virtual presentations for libraries, church groups, non-profits, businesses, or schools—typically, after engaging with the material, wanted to know if self-government was really possible.

Self-government is achievable! I hope by now you are convinced and that the background and insights I've provided help answer any questions you may have about dismantling the *Indian Act*. The process has already begun, and there's solid groundwork to build upon. Many examples of self-government agreements and constitutions are already in place, and we're seeing changes resulting from treaty negotiations, too.

When the *Indian Act* is fully dismantled, in the long run, we will have greater economic certainty and opportunities as we will be working with Indigenous governments chosen and supported by the people; there will be less vitriolic animosity, fewer missing and murdered Indigenous women and girls, and more transparent and accountable Indigenous governments, to name a few benefits.

From my decades of experience providing training and presentations, and writing blog articles and books on the *Indian Act*, self-government, and other Indigenous issues, I know that people see the problems of the *Indian Act* and want to contribute in some way to changing the *Indian Act* relationship by moving to self-government. I've seen firsthand that when people have their aha moments, they feel good about their current understanding. They see future opportunities for change (that can take this country to the next level in Indigenous relations) and the mutually beneficial relationships that will transpire.

Dismantling the *Indian Act* and moving faster to self-government arrangements will not be done using a cookie-cutter approach. There are many common elements of self-government agreements, such as the power to enact laws and establish government-to-government relationships. Each agreement will be done on a case-by-case basis, each community operating within its frame of reference.

Will self-government work? Plenty of agreements are already in place now, some that are very recent and some that have been around for a while, demonstrating that there are workable solutions. When we look at those agreements, the test I use to gauge if they are working is whether they are being discussed on the evening news. They are working if we don't hear much about them.

While complete self-government may sound expensive and impossible to afford, given the current economy, the reality is that Canada is already spending a significant amount of money on *Indian Act* programs such as health care, housing, and education. These programs will continue, but the funding may be allocated in ways that better align with community values and ideas, thereby making them more efficient and effective.

Dismantling the *Indian Act* will be good for the economy. First Nations communities with self-government agreements, constitutions, and clarity around citizenship and governance will be much more straightforward to work with. By these communities establishing self-governance, governments and developers can confidently identify and engage appropriate Indigenous representatives, streamlining consultation processes and upholding commitments to the UN Declaration on the Rights of Indigenous Peoples. This clarity fosters economic certainty and opportunities across Canada.

Access to capital markets will be an essential feature of dismantling the *Indian Act*. The ability for families to own their own homes and borrow money against those homes, to borrow money to fix things and buy businesses, and to do all that is available to other Canadians is a really important reason to move beyond the *Indian Act*.

Self-governing communities are looking to be more self-reliant, and the plan, as communities see it, is to be in a position to generate their own revenues through various activities. The vision is that these revenues will be put towards programs, services, and additional investment opportunities that will add more value to their quality of life.

All this activity sometimes makes us forget that communities are in a race against time to devise ways to dismantle the *Indian Act* and move to self-government. The *Indian Act* is still doing what it set out to do: removing people from the "list." We need more self-government now.

While the government of Canada moves towards more self-government agreements with Indigenous Peoples, the country will continue to have a fiduciary duty and legal obligation to First Nations. This obligation will remain on a government-to-government or nation-to-nation level, rather than on a government-to-individual level.

I APPRECIATE you taking the time to read this book and to expand your understanding of self-government and the process of dismantling the *Indian Act*. Your willingness to learn, share, and hopefully engage is so important to the process of change. I hope you'll feel inspired to join the conversation and help improve the quality of life for all Canadians. It's in reach: We only need to keep our foot on the gas pedal and move to Indigenous self-government sooner, rather than later.

APPENDIX I

Join the Conversation!

THE YEAR 2026 marks 150 years of the existence of the consolidated *Indian Act, 1876*. I expect that the place of the *Indian Act* in Canadian and Indigenous society will be brought under scrutiny. I hope that through this book you have seen that the move to self-government is not to be feared but encouraged. My hope is that you will consider joining the conversation. Here are some ideas on how to do so.

Online Conversations
Hashtag campaign—Use one of the following hashtags:

#IndianAct150
#IndigenousSelfGovernment
#BeyondTheIndianAct
#JoinTheConversation
#21Things
#IndigenousRelations
#DismantleTheIndianAct

And encourage people to share their thoughts, experiences, or questions.

Live Q&A sessions—Participate in live discussions on Instagram, LinkedIn, or YouTube where people are asking questions and contributing their perspectives.

Discussion group—Join a LinkedIn group where people are discussing dismantling the *Indian Act*.

Blog or video responses—Write a blog post or record a video to respond to ideas from this book and share it using one of the hashtags.

In-Person Events

Book clubs and reading circles—Join or form a book club and use ideas from this book as discussion points. Start discussions and reading circles with the groups and communities you belong to; talk about the themes from this book.

Workshops, training, and talks—Participate in or organize workplace learning or training sessions and workplace speaking engagements. Use ideas from this book for direction. Or attend the great offerings of libraries across the country.

Indigenous-led panels—Collaborate with Indigenous leaders, activists, or scholars for round table discussions.

Creative Participation

Story submissions—Invite people to share personal stories related to the *Indian Act* and its impact and post these on your social media page or organizational blog.

Art and poetry—Encourage artistic responses, such as visual art, spoken word, or poetry, to reflect on the themes in this book.

Podcasting—Feature guest interviews or questions submitted by listeners on a podcast episode discussing this book's themes.

Call to Action for Change

Petitions and advocacy—Encourage people to support existing movements working to dismantle the *Indian Act*.

Letter-writing campaigns—Provide your community with templates for letters people can send to government officials advocating for change. A key change would be for parliamentarians to get all-party support for legislative changes.

Policy dialogue—Help people draft thoughtful questions to raise with elected officials or community leaders.

Personal Actions

- Do your own research on the *Indian Act* and the process of dismantling it under way now.

- Learn about the United Nations Declaration on the Rights of Indigenous Peoples.

- Use the Indigenous Corporate Training Inc. RESPECT™ model to learn about the Indigenous Peoples close to you.[1] You can learn about this model in the Indigenous Relations or *Working Effectively with Indigenous Peoples*® training courses.

- Pick one of the Calls to Action from the Truth and Reconciliation Commission and pursue the prescribed action.

APPENDIX 2

Questions from Indigenous Youth

IN 2023, I was invited by Elder Whabagoon, co-founder and co-leader of Nikibii Dawadinna Giigwag,[1] a program at the University of Toronto that connects Indigenous youth with traditional teachings on the land, to speak to the members of this group.

After my talk, we discussed their concerns regarding their future and the future of Canada. The questions were so inspirational and provided so much insight into the minds of Indigenous youth that I decided to include many of the questions here.

These questions can be used to test your knowledge or to initiate classroom discussions, or as a basis for a workplace reconciliation workshop. I have given my own answers to some of the questions from the youth in this book (specifically, questions 1, 4, 5, and 11). Other questions are for your consideration, and my hope is that you use them to continue your learning journey. I know I will be using them to continue my own learning journey and hope to provide answers on the *Working Effectively with Indigenous Peoples*® blog in the future.

1. What is your perspective on the *Indian Act* from the past until now?

2. How can Indigenous youth engage in the renewal of their cultural identity?

3. Do you think that the final act of reconciliation is returning all the land?

4. What are the benefits and losses of repealing the *Indian Act*?

5. When did settlers stop viewing us as Nations, and why?

6. Was then Prime Minister Stephen Harper's 2008 apology[2] on behalf of Canada for the Indian residential school system authentic? (See chapter 5 in *21 Things You May Not Know About the Indian Act*.) Do you think an apology should be followed by actions?

7. Do you believe blood quantum is a valid way of determining a person's status as Indigenous?

8. How would you help individuals who struggle with Indigenous identity?

9. Do you think Canada should have a third level of government governed by Indigenous Peoples?

10. What are your thoughts on the debate about some Indigenous art not being Indigenous enough?

11. What is your vision for the future of Canada?

APPENDIX 3

Additional Reading

I ENCOURAGE YOU to visit the website of a self-governing Nation and read its Agreement. As you read the General Provisions or whatever terminology the agreement uses, think about the reasoning behind what is included and why it is a priority. If you read only one agreement, I recommend you read the Nisga'a Final Agreement, available at nisgaanation.ca/government/nisgaa-treaty.

Below are a few books that I believe will further your knowledge of Indigenous relations.

Arthur Manuel and Grand Chief Ronald M. Derrickson, *Unsettling Canada: A National Wake-Up Call* (Between the Lines, 2015).
Bob Joseph, *21 Things You May Not Know About the Indian Act: Helping Canadians Make Reconciliation with Indigenous Peoples a Reality* (Indigenous Relations Press, 2018).
Bob Joseph and Cynthia F. Joseph, *Working Effectively with Indigenous Peoples®*, 4th ed. (Indigenous Relations Press, 2017).
Bob Joseph with Cynthia F. Joseph, *Indigenous Relations: Insights, Tips, and Suggestions to Make Reconciliation a Reality* (Indigenous Relations Press, 2019).

Calvin Helin, *Dances with Dependency: Out of Poverty Through Self-Reliance* (Cubbie Blue Publishing, 2008).

Harold R. Johnson, *Peace and Good Order: The Case for Indigenous Justice in Canada* (McClelland & Stewart, 2023).

Jessica McDiarmid, *Highway of Tears: A True Story of Racism, Indifference and the Pursuit of Justice for Missing and Murdered Indigenous Women and Girls* (Anchor Canada, 2020).

Jody Wilson-Raybould and Roshan Danesh, *Reconciling History: A Story of Canada* (McClelland & Stewart, 2024).

Michelle Good, *Truth Telling: Seven Conversations About Indigenous Life in Canada* (HarperCollins Publishers, 2023).

Tanya Talaga, *Seven Fallen Feathers: Racism, Death, and Hard Truths in a Northern City* (House of Anansi Press, 2017) and *The Knowing* (HarperCollins Publishers, 2024).

Thomas King, *The Truth About Stories: A Native Narrative* (House of Anansi Press, 2003) and *The Inconvenient Indian: A Curious Account of Native People in North America* (Anchor Canada, 2013).

Truth and Reconciliation Commission of Canada, *Honouring the Truth, Reconciling for the Future: Summary of the Final Report of the Truth and Reconciliation Commission of Canada* (Truth and Reconciliation Commission of Canada, 2015).

APPENDIX 4

United Nations Declaration on the Rights of Indigenous Peoples

Article 1

Indigenous peoples have the right to the full enjoyment, as a collective or as individuals, of all human rights and fundamental freedoms as recognized in the Charter of the United Nations, the Universal Declaration of Human Rights and international human rights law.

Article 2

Indigenous peoples and individuals are free and equal to all other peoples and individuals and have the right to be free from any kind of discrimination, in the exercise of their rights, in particular that based on their indigenous origin or identity.

Article 3

Indigenous peoples have the right to self-determination. By virtue of that right they freely determine their political status and freely pursue their economic, social and cultural development.

Article 4

Indigenous peoples, in exercising their right to self-determination, have the right to autonomy or self-government in matters relating to their internal and local affairs, as well as ways and means for financing their autonomous functions.

Article 5

Indigenous peoples have the right to maintain and strengthen their distinct political, legal, economic, social and cultural institutions, while retaining their right to participate fully, if they so choose, in the political, economic, social and cultural life of the State.

Article 6

Every indigenous individual has the right to a nationality.

Article 7

1 Indigenous individuals have the rights to life, physical and mental integrity, liberty and security of person.

2 Indigenous peoples have the collective right to live in freedom, peace and security as distinct peoples and shall not be subjected to any act of genocide or any other act of violence, including forcibly removing children of the group to another group.

Article 8

1 Indigenous peoples and individuals have the right not to be subjected to forced assimilation or destruction of their culture.

2 States shall provide effective mechanisms for prevention of, and redress for:

   (a) Any action which has the aim or effect of depriving them of their integrity as distinct peoples, or of their cultural values or ethnic identities;

   (b) Any action which has the aim or effect of dispossessing them of their lands, territories or resources;

   (c) Any form of forced population transfer which has the aim or effect of violating or undermining any of their rights;

   (d) Any form of forced assimilation or integration;

   (e) Any form of propaganda designed to promote or incite racial or ethnic discrimination directed against them.

Article 9

Indigenous peoples and individuals have the right to belong to an indigenous community or nation, in accordance with the traditions and customs of the community or nation concerned. No discrimination of any kind may arise from the exercise of such a right.

Article 10

Indigenous peoples shall not be forcibly removed from their lands or territories. No relocation shall take place without the free, prior and informed consent of the indigenous peoples concerned and after agreement on just and fair compensation and, where possible, with the option of return.

Article 11

1 Indigenous peoples have the right to practise and revitalize their cultural traditions and customs. This includes the right to maintain, protect and develop the past, present and future manifestations of their cultures, such as archaeological and historical sites, artefacts, designs, ceremonies, technologies and visual and performing arts and literature.

2 States shall provide redress through effective mechanisms, which may include restitution, developed in conjunction with indigenous peoples, with respect to their cultural, intellectual, religious and spiritual property taken without their free, prior and informed consent or in violation of their laws, traditions and customs.

Article 12

1 Indigenous peoples have the right to manifest, practise, develop and teach their spiritual and religious traditions, customs and ceremonies; the right to maintain, protect, and have access in privacy to their religious and cultural sites; the right to the use and control of their ceremonial objects; and the right to the repatriation of their human remains.

2   States shall seek to enable the access and/or repatriation of ceremonial objects and human remains in their possession through fair, transparent and effective mechanisms developed in conjunction with indigenous peoples concerned.

Article 13

1   Indigenous peoples have the right to revitalize, use, develop and transmit to future generations their histories, languages, oral traditions, philosophies, writing systems and literatures, and to designate and retain their own names for communities, places and persons.

2   States shall take effective measures to ensure that this right is protected and also to ensure that indigenous peoples can understand and be understood in political, legal and administrative proceedings, where necessary through the provision of interpretation or by other appropriate means.

Article 14

1   Indigenous peoples have the right to establish and control their educational systems and institutions providing education in their own languages, in a manner appropriate to their cultural methods of teaching and learning.

2   Indigenous individuals, particularly children, have the right to all levels and forms of education of the State without discrimination.

3 States shall, in conjunction with indigenous peoples, take effective measures, in order for indigenous individuals, particularly children, including those living outside their communities, to have access, when possible, to an education in their own culture and provided in their own language.

Article 15

1 Indigenous peoples have the right to the dignity and diversity of their cultures, traditions, histories and aspirations which shall be appropriately reflected in education and public information.

2 States shall take effective measures, in consultation and cooperation with the indigenous peoples concerned, to combat prejudice and eliminate discrimination and to promote tolerance, understanding and good relations among indigenous peoples and all other segments of society.

Article 16

1 Indigenous peoples have the right to establish their own media in their own languages and to have access to all forms of non-indigenous media without discrimination.

2 States shall take effective measures to ensure that State-owned media duly reflect indigenous cultural diversity. States, without prejudice to ensuring full freedom of expression, should encourage privately owned media to adequately reflect indigenous cultural diversity.

Article 17

1 Indigenous individuals and peoples have the right to enjoy fully all rights established under applicable international and domestic labour law.

2 States shall in consultation and cooperation with indigenous peoples take specific measures to protect indigenous children from economic exploitation and from performing any work that is likely to be hazardous or to interfere with the child's education, or to be harmful to the child's health or physical, mental, spiritual, moral or social development, taking into account their special vulnerability and the importance of education for their empowerment.

3 Indigenous individuals have the right not to be subjected to any discriminatory conditions of labour and, inter alia, employment or salary.

Article 18

Indigenous peoples have the right to participate in decision-making in matters which would affect their rights, through representatives chosen by themselves in accordance with their own procedures, as well as to maintain and develop their own indigenous decision-making institutions.

Article 19

States shall consult and cooperate in good faith with the indigenous peoples concerned through their own representative institutions in order to obtain their free, prior and informed consent before adopting and implementing legislative or administrative measures that may affect them.

Article 20

1 Indigenous peoples have the right to maintain and develop their political, economic and social systems or institutions, to be secure in the enjoyment of their own means of subsistence and development, and to engage freely in all their traditional and other economic activities.

2 Indigenous peoples deprived of their means of subsistence and development are entitled to just and fair redress.

Article 21

1 Indigenous peoples have the right, without discrimination, to the improvement of their economic and social conditions, including, inter alia, in the areas of education, employment, vocational training and retraining, housing, sanitation, health and social security.

2 States shall take effective measures and, where appropriate, special measures to ensure continuing improvement of their economic and social conditions. Particular attention shall be paid to the rights and special needs of indigenous elders, women, youth, children and persons with disabilities.

Article 22

1 Particular attention shall be paid to the rights and special needs of indigenous elders, women, youth, children and persons with disabilities in the implementation of this Declaration.

2 States shall take measures, in conjunction with indigenous peoples, to ensure that indigenous women and children enjoy the full protection and guarantees against all forms of violence and discrimination.

Article 23

Indigenous peoples have the right to determine and develop priorities and strategies for exercising their right to development. In particular, indigenous peoples have the right to be actively involved in developing and determining health, housing and other economic and social programmes affecting them and, as far as possible, to administer such programmes through their own institutions.

Article 24

1 Indigenous peoples have the right to their traditional medicines and to maintain their health practices, including the conservation of their vital medicinal plants, animals and minerals. Indigenous individuals also have the right to access, without any discrimination, to all social and health services.

2 Indigenous individuals have an equal right to the enjoyment of the highest attainable standard of physical and mental health. States shall take the necessary steps with a view to achieving progressively the full realization of this right.

Article 25

Indigenous peoples have the right to maintain and strengthen their distinctive spiritual relationship with their traditionally owned or otherwise occupied and used lands, territories, waters and coastal seas and other resources and to uphold their responsibilities to future generations in this regard.

Article 26

1 Indigenous peoples have the right to the lands, territories and resources which they have traditionally owned, occupied or otherwise used or acquired.

2 Indigenous peoples have the right to own, use, develop and control the lands, territories and resources that they possess by reason of traditional ownership or other traditional occupation or use, as well as those which they have otherwise acquired.

3 States shall give legal recognition and protection to these lands, territories and resources. Such recognition shall be conducted with due respect to the customs, traditions and land tenure systems of the indigenous peoples concerned.

Article 27

States shall establish and implement, in conjunction with indigenous peoples concerned, a fair, independent, impartial, open and transparent process, giving due recognition to indigenous peoples' laws, traditions, customs and land tenure systems, to recognize and adjudicate the rights of indigenous peoples pertaining to their lands, territories and resources, including those which were traditionally owned or otherwise occupied or used. Indigenous peoples shall have the right to participate in this process.

Article 28

1 Indigenous peoples have the right to redress, by means that can include restitution or, when this is not possible, just, fair and equitable compensation, for the lands, territories and resources which they have traditionally owned or otherwise occupied or used, and which have been confiscated, taken, occupied, used or damaged without their free, prior and informed consent.

2 Unless otherwise freely agreed upon by the peoples concerned, compensation shall take the form of lands, territories and resources equal in quality, size and legal status or of monetary compensation or other appropriate redress.

Article 29

1 Indigenous peoples have the right to the conservation and protection of the environment and the productive capacity of their lands or territories and resources. States shall establish and implement assistance programmes for indigenous peoples for such conservation and protection, without discrimination.

2 States shall take effective measures to ensure that no storage or disposal of hazardous materials shall take place in the lands or territories of indigenous peoples without their free, prior and informed consent.

3 States shall also take effective measures to ensure, as needed, that programmes for monitoring, maintaining and restoring the health of indigenous peoples, as developed and implemented by the peoples affected by such materials, are duly implemented.

Article 30

1 Military activities shall not take place in the lands or territories of indigenous peoples, unless justified by a relevant public interest or otherwise freely agreed with or requested by the indigenous peoples concerned.

2 States shall undertake effective consultations with the indigenous peoples concerned, through appropriate procedures and in particular through their representative institutions, prior to using their lands or territories for military activities.

Article 31

1 Indigenous peoples have the right to maintain, control, protect and develop their cultural heritage, traditional knowledge and traditional cultural expressions, as well as the manifestations of their sciences, technologies and cultures, including human and genetic resources, seeds, medicines, knowledge of the properties of fauna and flora, oral traditions, literatures, designs, sports and traditional games and visual and performing arts. They also have the right to maintain, control, protect and develop their intellectual property over such cultural heritage, traditional knowledge, and traditional cultural expressions.

2 In conjunction with indigenous peoples, States shall take effective measures to recognize and protect the exercise of these rights.

Article 32

1 Indigenous peoples have the right to determine and develop priorities and strategies for the development or use of their lands or territories and other resources.

2 States shall consult and cooperate in good faith with the indigenous peoples concerned through their own representative institutions in order to obtain their free and informed consent prior to the approval of any project affecting their lands or territories and other resources, particularly in connection with the development, utilization or exploitation of mineral, water or other resources.

3 States shall provide effective mechanisms for just and fair redress for any such activities, and appropriate measures shall be taken to mitigate adverse environmental, economic, social, cultural or spiritual impact.

Article 33

1 Indigenous peoples have the right to determine their own identity or membership in accordance with their customs and traditions. This does not impair the right of indigenous individuals to obtain citizenship of the States in which they live.

2 Indigenous peoples have the right to determine the structures and to select the membership of their institutions in accordance with their own procedures.

Article 34

Indigenous peoples have the right to promote, develop and maintain their institutional structures and their distinctive customs, spirituality, traditions, procedures, practices and, in the cases where they exist, juridical systems or customs, in accordance with international human rights standards.

Article 35

Indigenous peoples have the right to determine the responsibilities of individuals to their communities.

Article 36

1 Indigenous peoples, in particular those divided by international borders, have the right to maintain and develop contacts, relations and cooperation, including activities for spiritual, cultural, political, economic and social purposes, with their own members as well as other peoples across borders.

2 States, in consultation and cooperation with indigenous peoples, shall take effective measures to facilitate the exercise and ensure the implementation of this right.

Article 37

1 Indigenous peoples have the right to the recognition, observance and enforcement of treaties, agreements and other constructive arrangements concluded with States or their successors and to have States honour and respect such treaties, agreements and other constructive arrangements.

2 Nothing in this Declaration may be interpreted as diminishing or eliminating the rights of indigenous peoples contained in treaties, agreements and other constructive arrangements.

Article 38
States in consultation and cooperation with indigenous peoples, shall take the appropriate measures, including legislative measures, to achieve the ends of this Declaration.

Article 39
Indigenous peoples have the right to have access to financial and technical assistance from States and through international cooperation, for the enjoyment of the rights contained in this Declaration.

Article 40
Indigenous peoples have the right to access to and prompt decision through just and fair procedures for the resolution of conflicts and disputes with States or other parties, as well as to effective remedies for all infringements of their individual and collective rights. Such a decision shall give due consideration to the customs, traditions, rules and legal systems of the indigenous peoples concerned and international human rights.

Article 41
The organs and specialized agencies of the United Nations system and other intergovernmental organizations shall contribute to the full realization of the provisions of this Declaration through the mobilization, inter alia, of

financial cooperation and technical assistance. Ways and means of ensuring participation of indigenous peoples on issues affecting them shall be established.

Article 42

The United Nations, its bodies, including the Permanent Forum on Indigenous Issues, and specialized agencies, including at the country level, and States shall promote respect for and full application of the provisions of this Declaration and follow up the effectiveness of this Declaration.

Article 43

The rights recognized herein constitute the minimum standards for the survival, dignity and well-being of the indigenous peoples of the world.

Article 44

All the rights and freedoms recognized herein are equally guaranteed to male and female indigenous individuals.

Article 45

Nothing in this Declaration may be construed as diminishing or extinguishing the rights indigenous peoples have now or may acquire in the future.

Article 46

1 Nothing in this Declaration may be interpreted as implying for any State, people, group or person any right to engage in any activity or to perform any act contrary to the Charter of the United Nations or

construed as authorizing or encouraging any action which would dismember or impair, totally or in part, the territorial integrity or political unity of sovereign and independent States.

2 In the exercise of the rights enunciated in the present Declaration, human rights and fundamental freedoms of all shall be respected. The exercise of the rights set forth in this Declaration shall be subject only to such limitations as are determined by law and in accordance with international human rights obligations. Any such limitations shall be non-discriminatory and strictly necessary solely for the purpose of securing due recognition and respect for the rights and freedoms of others and for meeting the just and most compelling requirements of a democratic society.

3 The provisions set forth in this Declaration shall be interpreted in accordance with the principles of justice, democracy, respect for human rights, equality, non-discrimination, good governance and good faith.

Acknowledgements

I WOULD LIKE to acknowledge and thank all those who have helped in the creation of this book.

I am grateful to Jamie Broadhurst, Vice-President of Marketing at Raincoast Books, and Trena White, co-CEO of Page Two, for their encouragement to write a sequel to *21 Things You May Not Know About the Indian Act*.

I would like to acknowledge all those who contributed their time and expertise to this book. I want to recognize Julie Domvile, who played an essential role in writing and editing in both of the 21 Things books. A tip of the hat is in order to the people from Page Two for their support, guidance, and expertise: Kendra Ward, for guiding content development; Rony Ganon, for keeping us on track; and Peter Cocking, for his attention-grabbing cover art.

I also want to acknowledge the contributions of and share my gratitude to my remarkable team at Indigenous Corporate Training Inc.: Laura Bock, for her efforts in research, writing, and editing; Jane Wright, for research and editing; and Cindy Joseph, for doing everything, including and especially what I don't want to do or am not good at.

Notes

Epigraph

ix Special Committees of the Senate and House of Commons, *Meeting in Joint Session to Inquire into the Claims of the Allied Indian Tribes of British Columbia, as Set Forth in Their Petition Submitted to Parliament in June 1926*, 1st sess., 16th Parliament, April 4, 1927, vol. 1 (F.A. Acland, Printer to the King's Most Excellent Majesty, 1927), 160.

Introduction

1 Bob Joseph, *21 Things You May Not Know About the Indian Act: Helping Canadians Make Reconciliation with Indigenous Peoples a Reality* (Indigenous Relations Press, 2018).

From Royal Proclamation to Forced Assimilation

1 George R, Proclamation, 7 October 1763, reprinted in RSC 1985, App II, No. 1.
2 The Right Honourable Beverley McLachlin, PC, "Reconciling Unity and Diversity in the Modern Era: Tolerance and Intolerance," Annual Pluralism Lecture 2015 at the Global Centre for Pluralism, Ottawa, May 28, 2015.
3 *Constitution Act, 1867* (UK), 30 & 31 Vict, c. 3.
4 Robert Boyd, "Commentary on Early Contact-Era Smallpox in the Pacific Northwest," *Ethnohistory* 43, no. 2 (Spring 1996): 307–28.

5   C. Stuart Houston and Stan Houston, "The First Smallpox Epidemic on the Canadian Plains: In the Fur-Traders' Words," *Canadian Journal of Infectious Diseases and Medical Microbiology* 11, no. 2 (April 1, 2000): 112–15.
6   Elizabeth A. Fenn, "The Great Smallpox Epidemic," *History Today* 53, no. 8 (August 2003), historytoday.com/archive/great-smallpox-epidemic.
7   Houston and Houston, "The First Smallpox Epidemic."
8   Greg Lange, "Smallpox Epidemic of 1862 Among Northwest Coast and Puget Sound Indians," HistoryLink.org, February 4, 2003, historylink.org/File/5171.
9   The Canadian Press, "First Nations, Developer Call for Return and Protection of Sacred Burial Site in Abbotsford," *Vancouver Sun*, June 14, 2019, vancouversun.com/news/local-news/first-nations-developer-call-for-return-and-protection-of-sacred-burial-site-in-abbotsford.
10 Joshua Ostroff, "How a Smallpox Epidemic Forged Modern British Columbia," *Maclean's*, August 1, 2017, macleans.ca/news/canada/how-a-smallpox-epidemic-forged-modern-british-columbia.
11 *Annual Report of the Department of the Interior for the Year Ended 30th June, 1876* (Ottawa: Maclean, Roger & Co., 1877), xiv.
12 Peter H. Bryce, *Report on the Indian Schools of Manitoba and the Northwest Territories* (Government Printing Bureau, 1907).
13 Indian and Northern Affairs Canada, *Statement of the Government of Canada on Indian Policy*, 1969.
14 *Constitution Act, 1982*, being Schedule B to the *Canada Act 1982* (UK), 1982, c. 11, s. 35.
15 *Constitution Act, 1867* (UK), 30 & 31 Vict, c. 3, s. 91(24).

We Are Simply Dependent

1   Special Committees of the Senate and House of Commons, *Meeting in Joint Session to Inquire into the Claims of the Allied Indian Tribes of British Columbia*, 160.
2   *Constitution Act, 1867* (UK), 30 & 31 Vict, c. 3, s. 91(24).
3   Calvin Helin, *Dances with Dependency: Out of Poverty Through Self-Reliance* (Ravencrest Publishing, 2008).

What Is Self-Government?

1. Nisga'a Final Agreement (May 11, 2000).
2. *Calder et al. v. Attorney-General of British Columbia*, [1973], SCR 313.
3. In Canada and in this book, Indigenous Peoples includes First Nation ("Indian"), Inuit, and Métis Peoples. For all legal references, such as to rights and title, the term "Aboriginal" is used. Defined in the *Constitution Act, 1982*, Aboriginal Peoples includes all Indigenous Peoples in Canada: Status Indians, non-Status Indians, Métis, and Inuit.
4. Erin Hanson, "Aboriginal Title," Indigenous Foundations, accessed November 12, 2024, indigenousfoundations.arts.ubc.ca/aboriginal_title.
5. See "The Inherent Right to Self-Government Is a Section 35 Right" in Part I of "The Government of Canada's Approach to Implementation of the Inherent Right and the Negotiation of Aboriginal Self-Government," Government of Canada, last modified March 1, 2023.
6. Bill S-212, *An Act Providing for the Recognition of Self-Governing First Nations of Canada*, 1st sess., 41st Parliament, 2012.
7. Crown-Indigenous Relations and Northern Affairs Canada, "Self-Government," last modified March 18, 2024, rcaanc-cirnac.gc.ca/eng/1100100032275/1529354547314.
8. James Bay and Northern Quebec Agreement (November 11, 1975).
9. "Main Agreements of the Cree Nation Government," Cree Nation Government, accessed November 20, 2024, cngov.ca/governance-structure/legislation/agreements.
10. This quote is from the following article, which was adapted from a speech given by Joseph Gosnell in 2003, at the Harvard Faculty Club in Cambridge, Massachusetts: "A First Nation, Again: The Return of Self-Government and Self-Reliance in Canada's Nisga'a Nation," in "Shamanisms and Survival," *Cultural Survival Quarterly* 27, no. 2 (June 2003).
11. Westbank First Nation Self-Government Agreement (April 1, 2005).

12 "About Westbank First Nation," Westbank First Nation, accessed April 11, 2025, wfn.ca/our-community/about-westbank-first-nation.htm.

13 *Canadian Human Rights Act*, RSC 1985, c. H-6.

1. The United Nations Declaration on the Rights of Indigenous Peoples Sets the Standard

1 *What We Have Learned: Principles of Truth and Reconciliation* (Truth and Reconciliation Commission of Canada, 2015), 3.

2 United Nations Declaration on the Rights of Indigenous Peoples, A Res 61/295, UNGAOR, 61st Sess, Supp No 53, UN Doc A/RES/61/295 (2007), art. 43.

3 Indian and Northern Affairs Canada, "Canada Endorses the United Nations Declaration on the Rights of Indigenous Peoples," news release, November 12, 2010.

4 Indigenous and Northern Affairs Canada, "Canada Becomes a Full Supporter of the United Nations Declaration on the Rights of Indigenous Peoples," news release, May 10, 2016.

5 *United Nations Declaration on the Rights of Indigenous Peoples Act*, SC 2021, c. 14.

6 Karine Duhamel, "The United Nations Declaration on the Rights of Indigenous Peoples: The Struggle to Recognize Indigenous Rights in Canadian Law," Canadian Museum for Human Rights, September 8, 2022, humanrights.ca/story/the-united-nations-declaration-on-the-rights-of-indigenous-peoples.

2. Treaties and Self-Government Differ but Relate

1 Menno Boldt, *Surviving as Indians: The Challenge of Self-Government* (University of Toronto Press, 1993), 41.

2 Boldt, *Surviving as Indians*, 42.

3 Joseph, *21 Things You May Not Know About the Indian Act*, 73–74.

4 Immigration, Refugees and Citizenship Canada, "INAN—Section 35 of the *Constitution Act, 1982*—Background—Jan 28, 2021," last modified May 13, 2021,

canada.ca/en/immigration-refugees-citizenship/corporate/transparency/committees/inan-jan-28-2021/inan-section-35-consitution-act-1982-background-jan-28-2021.html.
5 Crown-Indigenous Relations and Northern Affairs Canada, "Self-Government."
6 Treaty No. 8, signed June 21, 1899.
7 *shíshálh Nation Self-Government Act*, SC 1986, c. 27 (amended in 2022, c. 9).
8 Westbank First Nation Self-Government Agreement (April 1, 2005); Nisga'a Final Agreement (May 11, 2000).

3. Self-Government Aligns With Sovereignty

1 Harold Cardinal, *The Unjust Society* (Douglas & McIntyre, 1999), 11.

4. The Trustee-Wardship Relationship Dissolves

1 *Constitution Act, 1867* (UK), 30 & 31 Victoria, c. 3, s. 91(24).

5. Reserve Realities Change

1 Harvey McCue and Zach Parrott, "Canadian Aboriginal Reserves," Britannica, September 16, 2016.
2 Crown-Indigenous Relations and Northern Affairs Canada, "The Numbered Treaties (1871–1921)," last modified March 15, 2023, rcaanc-cirnac.gc.ca/eng/1360948213124/1544620003549.
3 "Laws," Westbank First Nation, accessed April 7, 2025, wfn.ca/your-government/law-enforcement/laws.htm.
4 "Lands Registry," Westbank First Nation, accessed April 7, 2025, wfn.ca/business-development/lands-registry.htm.

6. Laws of General Application Apply

1 Crown-Indigenous Relations and Northern Affairs Canada, *Nisga'a Final Agreement 2001 Annual Report*, 27, last modified September 15, 2010.
2 Nisga'a Final Agreement (May 11, 2000).
3 Anishinabek Nation Governance Agreement (April 6, 2022).

4 Anishinabek Nation Governance Agreement (April 6, 2022), s. 6.4.
5 Westbank First Nation Self-Government Agreement (April 1, 2005), s. 22(a) and s. 195.

7. Traditional Leadership Is Tied to Community

1 *Indian Act*, RSC 1985, c. I-5, s. 74(2).
2 "*Indian Act* and Elected Chief and Band Council System," Indigenous Corporate Training Inc., June 25, 2015, ictinc.ca/blog/indian-act-and-elected-chief-and-band-council-system.
3 "Hereditary Chief Definition and 5 FAQs," Indigenous Corporate Training Inc., March 1, 2016, ictinc.ca/blog/hereditary-chief-definition-and-5-faqs.
4 BC Treaty Commission, *The Self Government Landscape*, September 2002, bctreaty.ca/wp-content/uploads/2016/09/self_government_landscape.pdf.
5 Maa-nulth First Nations Final Agreement (April 1, 2011).
6 "About Us," Huu-ay-aht First Nations, accessed April 11, 2025, huuayaht.org/about/who-we-are.
7 Ta'an Kwach'an Council Self-Government Agreement (April 1, 2002).
8 A moiety system is a social structure that divides a society into two complementary parts that trace their ancestry through either the male or female line, but not both. Each part often has specific roles, responsibilities, and marriage regulations. It is similar to a clan system, but while clans can be made up of multiple groups and believe in descent from a common ancestor, moieties occur only in pairs and are related through marriage to those in both moieties, not by descent from a common ancestor.
9 Constitution of the Ta'an Kwäch'än Council, April 1, 2024, s. 8.
10 "The Journey to Gwayile'las," 'Namgis First Nation, February 23, 2024, engage.namgis.bc.ca/namgis-blended-governance/news_feed/project-news-and-updates.

8. Nations Have the Right to Choose Their People

1 "Guide to Membership Codes," Assembly of First Nations, Legal Affairs and Justice, March 31, 2020, afn.ca/wp-content/uploads/2020/11/20-03-31-Draft-Membership-Guide-final.pdf.
2 United Nations Declaration on the Rights of Indigenous Peoples, art. 33.
3 Constitution of the Haida Nation (October 18, 2023), art. 2.
4 Constitution of the Haida Nation (October 18, 2023), art. 2.S5.
5 Gwich'in Comprehensive Land Claim Agreement (April 10, 1992).
6 Gwich'in Comprehensive Land Claim Agreement (April 10, 1992), c. 4.

9. Nations Determine Their Financial Checks and Balances

1 Jackie McKay, "Lawsuit Alleges Corruption and Back Door Dealings at Key First Nation," CBC, November 29, 2024, cbc.ca/news/indigenous/key-first-nation-lawsuit-1.7382819.
2 Daphne Bramham, "First Nations Chiefs' Rich Lives Disrupted by Disclosure," *Vancouver Sun*, last updated August 24, 2015, vancouversun.com/news/metro/daphne-bramham-first-nations-chiefs-rich-lives-disrupted-by-disclosure; "The Chief of a Tiny B.C. First Nation with Only 39 Members Was Paid More Than $200,000," *National Post*, August 17, 2015, nationalpost.com/news/canada/the-chief-of-a-tiny-b-c-first-nation-with-only-39-members-was-paid-more-than-200000.
3 *First Nations Financial Transparency Act*, SC 2013, c. 7.
4 *First Nations Financial Transparency Act*, SC 2013, c. 7, s.3.
5 Indigenous and Northern Affairs Canada, "Statement by the Honourable Carolyn Bennett on the First Nations Financial Transparency Act," December 8, 2015.
6 Bill Curry, "Outgoing Chief," *Globe and Mail*, July 9, 2009, theglobeandmail.com/news/national/outgoing-chief/article4194579.
7 See "Accountability" in Part I of "The Government of Canada's Approach to Implementation of the Inherent Right and the Negotiation of Aboriginal Self-Government."

8 "About," Squamish Nation Constitution Project, accessed April 9, 2025, constitutionproject.net/about.
9 Tłı̨chǫ Land Claims and Self-Government Agreement (August 4, 2005), s. 7.1.2(c).
10 Tłı̨chǫ Constitution (August 13, 2000).
11 Tłı̨chǫ Government Administrative Policy and Procedures (August 25, 2003), revised July 24, 2024.

10. The Fiduciary Duty Diminishes

1 Crown-Indigenous Relations and Northern Affairs Canada, "Budget Management Principles," last modified February 1, 2019, isc-sac.gc.ca/eng/1549034289631/1584371125401.
2 Kevin Page, *Expert Analysis: Federal Funding and First Nations in Canada*, Institute of Fiscal Studies and Democracy, University of Ottawa, June 27, 2024.
3 *Status Report of the Auditor General of Canada to the House of Commons*, Chapter 4: Programs for First Nations on Reserves (Office of the Auditor General of Canada, 2011), 31–32.
4 Crown-Indigenous Relations and Northern Affairs Canada, "Self-Government."
5 Crown-Indigenous Relations and Northern Affairs Canada, "Canada's Collaborative Self-Government Fiscal Policy," last modified August 27, 2019, rcaanc-cirnac.gc.ca/eng/15664829 24303/1566482963919.
6 Sioux Valley Dakota Nation Governance Agreement and Tripartite Governance Agreement (July 1, 2014).
7 *Indian Act Amendment and Replacement Act*, SC 2014, c. 38.
8 Indigenous Services Canada, *Tenth Annual (2024) Statutory Report Pursuant to Section 2 of the Indian Act Amendment and Replacement Act, Statutes of Canada, Chapter 38, 2014*, last modified February 26, 2024.

11. Tax Is Included

1 Canada Revenue Agency, "Information on the Tax Exemption Under Section 87 of the *Indian Act*," last modified February 20, 2025, canada.ca/en/revenue-agency/services/indigenous-peoples/information-indians.html.

2 "Status Indians and Taxes," Indigenous Corporate Training Inc., May 5, 2014, ictinc.ca/blog/status-indians-and-taxes.
3 "Taxpayers: Property Taxation on Reserve," First Nations Tax Commission, accessed April 9, 2025, fntc.ca/property-taxation-on-reserve.
4 Tsawwassen First Nation Final Agreement (April 3, 2009).
5 Tsawwassen First Nation, *2023/2024 Annual Report*, n.d., tsawwassenfirstnation.com/pdfs/TFN-About/Information-Centre/Annual-Reports/2023-2024_Annual_Report_FINAL.pdf.

12. Indigenous Rights Include Language Rights

1 United Nations Declaration on the Rights of Indigenous Peoples, art. 11.
2 "Residential School History," National Centre for Truth and Reconciliation, University of Manitoba, accessed April 11, 2025, nctr.ca/education/teaching-resources/residential-school-history.
3 "Indigenous Languages Across Canada," Statistics Canada, last modified July 3, 2024, www12.statcan.gc.ca/census-recensement/2021/as-sa/98-200-x/2021012/98-200-x2021012-eng.cfm.
4 "Indigenous Languages Across Canada."
5 Rhiannon Russell, "First Nations Are Rethinking Education in the Yukon. And It's Working," *The Walrus*, last modified March 7, 2025, thewalrus.ca/first-nation-school-board.
6 Lauren-Rose Stunell, "Discovering Languages: Tłı̨chǫ and Language Revitalization Through Self-Government," Canadian Association of Second Language Teachers, March 11, 2025, caslt.org/en/blog-discovering-languages-tlicho/.
7 Kim Baird, Chris G. Buse, Kevin Hanna, Richard Krehbiel, and Karen Ogen, *Impact Benefit Agreements: Key Insights from First Nations', Government and Industry Leaders*, 13, First Nations Liquefied Natural Gas Alliance, last modified January 25, 2023, fnlngalliance.com/benefit-agreements.
8 "Raglan Agreement," Glencore Canada Corp., accessed April 9, 2025, glencore.ca/en/raglan/raglan-agreement.

9 "Raglan Education Fund," Glencore Canada Corp., accessed April 9, 2025, glencore.ca/en/raglan/sustainability/community/community-raglan-education-fund.

10 "Raglan Agreement: Celebrating 30 Years of Collaboration," Glencore Canada Corp., February 28, 2025, glencore.ca/en/raglan/News-and-Media/The-Raglan-Agreement--30-years-of-collaboration-and-innovation.

11 *Indigenous Languages Act*, SC 2019, c. 23, s. 6.

12 *Indigenous Languages Act*, SC 2019, c. 23, preamble.

13 Assembly of First Nations, First Nations Languages Funding Fact Sheet, August 2023, afn.bynder.com/m/1fa00c203bb77e39/original/Languages-Funding-Factsheet-2023.pdf.

13. Socio-Economic Issues Can Be Remedied

1 World Health Organization, *The Health of Indigenous Peoples*, WHA76.16, agenda item 16.3 at the 76th World Health Assembly, May 30, 2023, apps.who.int/gb/ebwha/pdf_files/WHA76/A76_R16-en.pdf.

2 Krista Schafte and Sean Bruna, "The Influence of Intergenerational Trauma on Epigenetics and Obesity in Indigenous Populations—A Scoping Review," *Epigenetics* 18, no. 1 (2023).

3 John Richards and Parisa Mahboubi, *Measuring Student Outcomes: The Case for Identifying Indigenous Students in Canada's PISA Sample* (C.D. Howe Institute, February 13, 2018), 1.

4 Métis Urban Housing Corporation, "Statistics Canada 2021 Census in Brief Response," accessed November 22, 2024, metishousing.ca/uploads/source/Stats_Can_Response.pdf.

5 "Indigenous Peoples—2021 Census Promotional Material," Statistics Canada, last modified February 1, 2023, statcan.gc.ca/en/census/census-engagement/community-supporter/indigenous-peoples; "An Update on the Socio-Economic Gaps Between Indigenous Peoples and the Non-Indigenous Population in Canada: Highlights from the 2021 Census," Statistics Canada, last modified October 25, 2023, sac-isc.gc.ca/eng/1690909773300/1690909797208.

6 "Aboriginal People Living Off-Reserve and the Labour Market: Estimates from the Labour Force Survey, 2007–2015," Statistics Canada, last modified March 27, 2017, statcan.gc.ca/n1/pub/71-588-x/71-588-x2017001-eng.htm.

7 "Higher Rates of Unemployment—#5 of 8 Key Issues," Indigenous Corporate Training Inc., May 2, 2023, ictinc.ca/blog/higher-rates-of-unemployment-5-of-8-key-issues.

8 Chris Beaver, "Why Are Indigenous People Over-Incarcerated in Canada?" TVO Today, June 13, 2024, tvo.org/article/why-are-indigenous-people-over-incarcerated-in-canada.

9 "Higher Rates of Death in Children and Youth—#7 of 8 Key Issues," Indigenous Corporate Training Inc., July 18, 2023, ictinc.ca/blog/higher-rates-of-death-in-children-and-youth-7-of-8-key-issues.

10 "Suicide Prevention in Indigenous Communities," Indigenous Services Canada, last modified May 3, 2024, sac-isc.gc.ca/eng/1576089685593/1576089741803.

11 "What We Do," Aboriginal Housing Management Association, accessed April 17, 2025, ahma-bc.org/about/what-we-do.

12 "Yukon First Nations Launch New, Independent Education Directorate," Council of Yukon First Nations, August 13, 2020, cyfn.ca/yukon-first-nations-launch-new-independent-education-directorate.

13 "About Us," Yukon First Nation Education Directorate, accessed April 10, 2025, yfned.ca/about-us.

14 "First Nation School Board," infographic, Yukon First Nation Education Directorate, accessed April 10, 2025, yfned.ca/fnsb.

15 *Nisga'a Final Agreement/Implementation Report 2021–2022* (Minister of Crown-Indigenous Relations; British Columbia's Ministry of Indigenous Relations and Reconciliation; and Nisga'a Lisims Government, 2022), nisgaanation.ca/wp-content/uploads/2025/01/NLG-AR2021-22-ENGLISH-WEB.pdf.

16 "Access to Justice Department," Nisga'a Lisims Government, accessed April 10, 2025, nisgaanation.ca/services/justice/access-to-justice-department.

14. The Infrastructure Gap Closes

1 Joe McFarland, "Schulich Professor Says Municipalities Around the World Are Learning Lessons from Calgary's 2024 Water Feeder Main Break," University of Calgary, January 7, 2025.
2 First Nations Finance Authority, *Reducing the Barriers to Indigenous Economic Growth: The First Nations Finance Authority and Monetization*, brief submitted to the House of Commons Standing Committee on Indigenous and Northern Affairs, February 2022, ourcommons.ca/Content/Committee/441/INAN/Brief/BR11559186/br-external/FirstNationsFinanceAuthority-e.pdf.
3 First Nations Finance Authority, *Reducing the Barriers*, 4–5.
4 "Moving Forward on Canada's National Infrastructure Assessment," Government of Canada, last modified December 3, 2024, housing-infrastructure.canada.ca/nia-eni/index-eng.html.
5 *Building Pathways to 2050: Moving Forward on the National Infrastructure Assessment* (Infrastructure Canada, 2021), 13.
6 *Building Pathways to 2050*, 13.
7 Tla'amin Final Agreement (signed April 11, 2014; in effect April 5, 2016).
8 "Short-Term Drinking Water Advisories," Indigenous Services Canada, last modified April 11, 2025, sac-isc.gc.ca/eng/1562856509704/1562856530304.
9 Kristine Liao, "61 Indigenous Communities in Canada Still Face Water Crisis," Global Poverty Project, Inc., September 30, 2020, globalcitizen.org/en/content/canada-indigenous-drinking-water-dangers; "Active Long-Term Drinking Water Advisories," Indigenous Services Canada, last modified March 11, 2025, sac-isc.gc.ca/eng/1614387410146/1614387435325.
10 Amanda Klasing, "Make It Safe: Canada's Obligation to End the First Nations Water Crisis," Human Rights Watch, June 7, 2016, hrw.org/report/2016/06/07/make-it-safe/canadas-obligation-end-first-nations-water-crisis.
11 "Who We Are," Neskantaga First Nation, accessed April 11, 2025, neskantaga.com/who-we-are.

12 "Neskantaga First Nation," Indigenous Services Canada, last modified August 23, 2024, sac-isc.gc.ca/eng/1614887856664/1614887885919.
13 "About Water and Sanitation: OHCHR and the Right to Water and Sanitation," United Nations Office of the High Commissioner for Human Rights, accessed April 11, 2025, ohchr.org/en/water-and-sanitation/about-water-and-sanitation.

15. Self-Reliance and Economic Reconciliation Can Begin with Small Actions

1 United Nations Declaration on the Rights of Indigenous Peoples, art. 21.1.
2 *Indian Act*, RSC 1985, c. I-5, s. 89(1).
3 "Statement by Chief Commissioner C.T. (Manny) Jules Regarding the First Nations Resource Charge," First Nations Tax Commission, January 30, 2023, fntc.ca/fnrc.
4 *First Nations Goods and Services Tax Act*, SC 2003, c. 15, s. 67.
5 Westbank First Nation, *Westbank First Nation Annual Report 2023/2024*, 17, accessed April 11, 2025, wfn.ca/docs/v2annual_report_2023_24_web.pdf.
6 "Statement by Chief Commissioner C.T. (Manny) Jules Regarding the First Nations Resource Charge."
7 Nisga'a Final Agreement (May 11, 2000), c. 5.
8 "Statement by Chief Commissioner C.T. (Manny) Jules Regarding the First Nations Resource Charge."
9 Jenny Higgins, "The Voisey's Bay Mine," Newfoundland and Labrador Heritage Website, accessed April 11, 2025, heritage.nf.ca/articles/economy/voiseys-bay.php.
10 David Keating, "August: Vale Unlocks the Next Phase of Voisey's Bay," *Canadian Mining Journal*, The Northern Miner Group, December 21, 2023.
11 "Voisey's Bay Mine, Guardians and a Path to Sustainability," Land Needs Guardians, last modified December 6, 2024, landneedsguardians.ca/resources/from-standoff-to-stewardship.
12 Government of British Columbia, "New Wind Projects Will Boost B.C.'s Affordable Clean-Energy Supply," news release,

December 9, 2024, news.gov.bc.ca/releases/2024ECS00
48-001643.
13 Bill S-268, *An Act to Amend the Criminal Code and the Indian Act*, 1st sess., 44th Parliament, 2023, summary (second reading 30 May 2024).
14 *Truth and Reconciliation Commission of Canada: Calls to Action* (Truth and Reconciliation Commission of Canada, 2015), 10.
15 "Hard Rock to Bolster Seminoles' Wealth," *The Columbus Dispatch*, April 7, 2007, dispatch.com/story/business/2007/04/07/hard-rock-to-bolster-seminoles/24226685007.
16 "Seminoles Today," Seminole Tribe of Florida, accessed April 17, 2025, semtribe.com/history/seminoles-today.

16. Free, Prior, and Informed Consent Must Be Obtained

1 United Nations Declaration on the Rights of Indigenous Peoples, art. 32.2.
2 *A Lay Person's Guide to Delgamuukw*, BC Treaty Commission, November 1999.
3 *Delgamuukw v. British Columbia* (1991), 79 DLR (4th) 185 (BCSC).
4 *Delgamuukw v. British Columbia* (1993), 104 DLR (4th) 479 (BCCA).
5 *Delgamuukw v. British Columbia* (1997), 3 SCR 1010.
6 "Why 2 Different Kinds of Wet'suwet'en Leaders Support and Oppose the Gas Pipeline," CBC, last modified February 20, 2020, cbc.ca/news/indigenous/blockade-railway-mowhak-wet-suwet-en-1.5467234.
7 Ayesha Habib, "The New Trans Mountain Pipeline Is Now Flowing. Could an Indigenous Rights Case Impact Operations?" The Narwhal News Society, last modified May 1, 2024, thenarwhal.ca/trans-mountain-launch-indigenous-rights.

17. Territories Can Overlap

1 "Negotiations Process," BC Treaty Commission, accessed April 11, 2025, bctreaty.ca/negotiations/negotiation-process.
2 "UBCIC Concerned That Recognition of Rights Policy for Treaty Negotiations in BC Privileges Only Some First Nations,"

Union of BC Indian Chiefs, news release, September 5, 2019, ubcic.bc.ca/ubcic_concerned_that_recognition_of_rights_policy_for_treaty_negotiations_in_bc_privileges_only_some_first_nations.

18. Self-Administration Is Not Self-Government

1 Duncan Campbell Scott quoted in Carol Anne Hilton, "Reconciliation Requires the Perpetrators' Truth as Well as the Victims'," *Policy Magazine*, September 30, 2021.
2 "Indigenous Services Canada," Government of Canada, last modified March 21, 2025, canada.ca/en/indigenous-services-canada.html.
3 Julie Williams, *Indian Act: Devolution and Opt-In Legislation*, 2, Shortcuts (briefings), Rebuilding First Nations Governance Project, Carleton University, September 2024.

19. Supporting Self-Government Is an Economic and Moral Opportunity

1 George R, Proclamation, 7 October 1763, reprinted in RSC 1985, App II, No. 1.
2 "A Fair Future for Indigenous Peoples," chapter 6 in *Budget 2024: Fairness for Every Generation* (Government of Canada, 2024), 269, budget.canada.ca/2024/report-rapport/chap6-en.html.
3 Hayden King and Riley Yesno, "Federal Budget 2024: An Indigenous Accounting," Yellowhead Institute, April 22, 2024.
4 Kamyar Razav, "The Feds Bought a Pipeline for $5B. How Did the Cost Balloon to over $30B?" Global News, August 9, 2023, globalnews.ca/news/9839473/trans-mountain-pipeline-cost-overrun.
5 *Canadian Human Rights Act*, RSC 1985, c. H-6.

20. Local Governments Can Support Self-Government

1 *Truth and Reconciliation Commission of Canada: Calls to Action*, 4.
2 ÁTOL,NEUEL ("Respecting One Another") Memorandum of Understanding Between the W̱SÁNEĆ Leadership Council Society and the District of Saanich (December 3, 2021).

3 "Haisla Nation," District of Kitimat, accessed November 28, 2024, kitimat.ca/en/our-community/haisla-nation.aspx.
4 "Reconciliation Contribution Fund," City of Victoria, accessed April 11, 2025, victoria.ca/city-government/reconciliation/reconciliation-contribution-fund.

Appendix 1: Join the Conversation!
1 Lauren Redman, "Susan Robertson: Building Indigenous Relationships with RESPECT™," Indigenous Corporate Training Inc., August 7, 2024, ictinc.ca/blog/susan-robertson-building-indigenous-relationships-with-respect.

Appendix 2: Questions from Indigenous Youth
1 "Nikibii Dawadinna Giigwag," Toronto and Region Conservation Authority, accessed April 11, 2025, trca.ca/learning/bolton-camp-project/nikibii-dawadinna-giigwag.
2 Crown-Indigenous Relations and Northern Affairs Canada, "Statement of Apology to Former Students of Indian Residential Schools," June 11, 2008.

Index

Aboriginal Housing Management Association (AHMA), 95
Aboriginal Peoples, use of term, 173n3. *See also* Indigenous Peoples
Aboriginal (Indigenous) Title, 14, 23, 38, 119, 121
accountability: financial, 67–70; leadership, 17–18
agriculture, 36, 45, 137
Anishinabek Nation Governance Agreement (2022), 50–51, 76, 102
Assembly of First Nations (AFN), 69
assimilation, 8–9, 10–12, 20, 43
Australia, 32

bands, 43, 54. *See also* Elected Chief and Council system
BC Hydro, 111–12
BC Treaty Commission, 119
Bill S-212 (*First Nations Self-Government Recognition Act*), 25
Bill S-268 (*An Act to Amend the Criminal Code and the Indian Act*), 112

Boldt, Menno, 36–37
British North America Act, 9, 18. See also *Constitution Act* (1867)
Building Pathways to 2050 (report), 101

Calder et al. v. Attorney General of British Columbia (1973), 22, 23, 35
Calgary, 99
Canada: Confederation, 8–9, 10, 18; *Constitution Act* (1867), 9, 12, 18, 21, 43; *Constitution Act* (1982), 8, 13–14, 38, 88, 173n3; federal spending on Indigenous Peoples, 71–73, 130, 141; fiduciary duty, 1, 12, 74, 76, 130, 142; UN Declaration and, 32. See also *Indian Act*
Canadian Charter of Rights and Freedoms, 26, 49, 63
Canadian Human Rights Act, 28, 132
Cardinal, Harold, 41–42
Charlottetown Accord (1992), 44
chiefs: Elected Chiefs, 18, 38, 53–54, 56, 67–68, 118–19, 122;

Hereditary Chiefs, 53, 54–55, 55–57, 58–60, 120, 122–23, 131
children and youth, 94
Chrétien, Jean (Chrétien government), 69
citizenship, 63–65. *See also* membership
Coastal GasLink pipeline project, 54–55, 122–23, 124, 131
Collaborative Self-Government Fiscal Policy, 74–76
colonization, 91, 125. See also *Indian Act*
comprehensive land claims (modern treaties), 35, 37–38
Confederation, 8–9, 10, 18
consent. *See* Free, Prior, and Informed Consent
Constitution Act (1867), 9, 12, 18, 21, 43
Constitution Act (1982), 8, 13–14, 38, 88, 173n3
consult, duty to, 119–20. *See also* Free, Prior, and Informed Consent
Coon Come, Matthew, 69
credit, 106–7, 141
Cree, 25–26, 42
Criminal Code, 49, 112
criminal justice system. *See* incarceration; justice
cultural genocide, 9
Curry, Bill, 69

death, of children and youth, 94
Delgamuukw v. British Columbia (1997), 119, 120–21
dependency, 18–19
drinking water advisories, 102–3

duty to consult, 119–20. *See also* Free, Prior, and Informed Consent

economic development: barriers to, 106, 107–8; credit and loans, 106–7, 141; economic certainty, 131; economic reconciliation and independence, 105–6, 112–14, 130; equity positions, 111–12; financial accountability and transparency, 67–70; gaming, 112; Impact and Benefit Agreements, 86–88, 110–11; joint projects with local government, 137; resource revenue sharing, 109–10; Seminole Tribe's example, 114–16; taxation, 79–81, 108–9. *See also* funding
education, 36, 72, 86, 88, 92–93, 95–96
Einstein, Albert, 94
Elected Chief and Council system, 18, 38, 53–54, 56, 67–68, 118–19, 122
emergency planning, 137
employment, 93, 111, 114
enfranchisement, 20
Environmental Protection Act, 49
equity positions, 111–12
Expert Analysis (federal funding report), 72

fiduciary duty, 1, 12, 74, 76, 130, 142
financial accountability and transparency, 67–70. *See also* economic development; funding

First Nation School Board (FNSB), 86, 96
First Nations Financial Transparency Act, 67–68
First Nations Goods and Services Tax (FNGST), 81, 108
First Nations LNG Alliance, 87
First Nations Resource Charge, 109–10
First Nations Self-Government Recognition Act (Bill S-212), 25
First Nations Tax Commission, 109
forestry stumpage fees, 109
Free, Prior, and Informed Consent, 117–24; about, 118–19; "Delgamuukw and Gisday'way" cases, 119, 120–21; duty to consult and, 119–20; resource extractive sector and, 117–18, 122–24; self-government and, 124; UN Declaration on, 117
funding: current principles and issues, 71–73, 130, 141; fiduciary duty, 1, 12, 74, 76, 130, 142; under self-government, 73–78. *See also* economic development

gaming, 112
genocide, cultural, 9
George III (king), 7–8, 129–30, 133
Gitxsan, 120–21
Gosnell, Joseph, 26–27
government-to-government relations, 38, 136, 140, 142. *See also* self-government
Grady, Glenn, 59
Gwich'in Comprehensive Land Claim Agreement (1992), 65

Haida Nation, 64–65
Haisla Nation Council, 137
health, 36, 72, 91
Helin, Calvin: *Dances with Dependency*, 18–19
Hereditary Chiefs, 53, 54–55, 55–57, 58–60, 120, 122–23, 131
housing, 46, 72, 93, 95
human rights, 103, 132–33. See also *Canadian Human Rights Act*; Indigenous Rights; United Nations Declaration on the Rights of Indigenous Peoples
Huu-ay-aht First Nations, 59

Impact and Benefit Agreements (IBAs), 86–88, 110–11
incarceration, 93–94. *See also* justice
income, 93, 114
income tax, 79–80, 81, 108
Indian Act: 1951 amendments, 61–62; assimilation goals and elimination of Status Indians, 10–11, 20, 127; "benefits" as restrictions, 20; credit and loan restrictions, 106–7; dependency from, 18–19, 44; dismantling, 1, 20, 44, 58, 76, 132, 139–42; Elected Chief and Council system, 18, 38, 53–54, 56, 67–68, 118–19, 122; financial accountability and, 70; human rights and, 132–33; legal representation prohibition, 37–38; membership restrictions, 20, 62–63, 64; Nisga'a and, 27; paradox of, 44; reconciliation and, 1; reserves and, 45;

taxes and, 79; UN Declaration and, 32–33; White Paper and, 12–13
Indian Act Amendment and Replacement Act, 76–78
Indigenous Corporate Training Inc., 11–12, 55
Indigenous Languages Act, 88
Indigenous Languages Program, 88. *See also* languages, Indigenous
Indigenous Peoples: assimilation and, 8–9, 10–12, 20, 43; Confederation and, 8–9, 10, 18; *Constitution Act* (1982) and, 8, 13–14, 38, 88, 173n3; death/injury of children and youth, 94; definition, 173n3; education, 36, 72, 86, 88, 92–93, 95–96; employment, 93, 111, 114; federal funding, 71–73, 130, 141; health, 36, 72, 91; housing, 46, 72, 93, 95; human rights and, 132–33; incarceration, 93–94; income and income tax, 79–80, 81, 93, 108, 114; litigation and negotiated settlements, 14–15; non-Status Indians, 64, 79, 80; residential schools, 11, 28, 84, 91; Royal Proclamation and, 7–8, 129–30; smallpox and, 9–10; Status Indians, 1, 20, 62, 79–80, 107, 133; suicide, 94; trustee-wardship relationship, 13, 14–15, 18, 43–44; White Paper and, 12–13. See also *Indian Act*; land; languages, Indigenous; leadership; reserves; self-government

Indigenous Rights, 7–8, 14, 88, 123. *See also* human rights; United Nations Declaration on the Rights of Indigenous Peoples
Indigenous Services Canada (ISC), 71–72, 77, 100, 127–28
Indigenous (Aboriginal) Title, 14, 23, 38, 119, 121
infrastructure, 99–102
injury, of children and youth, 94
Innu Nation, 111
Inuit, 80, 87–88, 111, 173n3

Jacob, Gibby, 130
James Bay and Northern Quebec Agreement (1975), 25–26, 76
Jules, C.T. (Manny), 108
justice, 50–51, 96–97. *See also* incarceration

Kangiqsujuaq (Inuit community), 87–88
Kelly, Peter, vii, 17
King, Hayden, 130
Kitimat, District of, 137
Ktunaxa, 57–58
Kwakwaka'wakw, 2, 65–66

Labrador Aboriginal Training Partnership, 111
Labrador Inuit Association (LIA), 111
land: comprehensive land claims (modern treaties), 35, 37–38; land use planning, 137; overlapping territories, 125–26; property taxes, 81, 109, 138; Traditional Territory, 54. *See also* reserves

languages, Indigenous: cultural significance, 84–85; local government support, 136; preservation and revitalization, 85–87, 88–89; residential schools and, 84; UN Declaration on, 83–84
laws of general application, 49–51
leadership: accountability and, 17–18; Elected Chiefs, 18, 38, 53–54, 56, 67–68, 118–19, 122; Hereditary Chiefs, 53, 54–55, 55–57, 58–60, 120, 122–23, 131; traditional, 53, 57–58
libraries, public, 136
litigation, 14–15
loans, 106–7, 141
local governments, 135–38

Maa-nulth First Nations Final Agreement (2011), 58–59
Macdonald, John A., 37
Makivik Corporation, 87–88
McEachern, Allan, 121
McLachlin, Beverley, 9
membership, 20, 61–63, 65–66. *See also* citizenship
Métis, 80, 173n3
mining. *See* resource extractive sector
missing and murdered Indigenous women, 62, 140
moiety system, 59, 176n8

names, 65–66
'Namgis Nation, 60
National Day for Truth and Reconciliation, 136
National Indigenous Peoples Day, 136

National Infrastructure Assessment, 101
Neskantaga First Nation, 103
New Zealand, 32
Nisga'a Final Agreement (2000), 21, 26–27, 39
Nisga'a Nation, 23, 49–50, 96–97, 109
non-Status Indians, 64, 79, 80. *See also* Indigenous Peoples
Numbered Treaties, 45–46
Nunatsiavut Guardians, 111

Osceola, Max, Jr., 114

Pierre, Sophie, 57–58
policing. *See* justice
Potlatch, 65–66
prisons, 93–94. *See also* justice
property taxes, 81, 109, 138

Quebec, 42

Raglan Agreement (1995), 87–88
real estate. *See* reserves
reconciliation: economic, 105–6, 112–14, 130; *Indian Act* and, 1; UN Declaration and, 33; Victoria's Reconciliation Contribution Fund, 138
Reducing the Barriers to Indigenous Economic Growth (report), 100–101
reserves: about, 45–46; drinking water advisories, 102–3; human rights and, 132–33; infrastructure, 99–102; real estate restrictions, 46–47, 106–7; self-government and, 47–48;

tax exemption and, 79–80;
White Paper and, 12. *See also*
Elected Chief and Council
system
residential schools, 11, 28, 84, 91
resource extractive sector, 86–88,
117–18, 122–24, 131
resource management partnerships, 137
resource revenue sharing, 109–10
rights. *See* human rights;
Indigenous Rights; United
Nations Declaration on the
Rights of Indigenous Peoples
Royal Proclamation (1763), 7–8,
129–30

Saanich, District of, 136
Salluit (Inuit community), 87–88
Scott, Duncan Campbell, 127
self-administration, 127–28
self-determination, 1–2, 33, 65–66,
76–78
self-government: introduction,
1–3, 21–22, 38; as achievable,
139–42; *Calder* case, 22, 23; citizenship and, 63–65; comparison
to self-administration, 127–28;
comparison to treaties, 38–39;
current state of, 25; financial
accountability and transparency under, 69–70; Free, Prior,
and Informed Consent and,
124; funding under, 73–78;
Hereditary Chiefs and, 58–60;
hesitation to embrace, 17–18,
19; individualized approach
to, 28, 140; infrastructure and,
101–2; as inherent right, 24–25;
language revitalization and, 89;
laws of general application and,
49–51; local government support
for, 135–38; reserves and,
47–48; Royal Proclamation and,
129–30; socio-economic issues
and, 94–97; sovereignty and,
41–42; taxes under, 80–81; traditional leadership and, 53, 57–58;
trustee-wardship relationship
and, 43–44; UN Declaration
and, 33
—SPECIFIC AGREEMENTS:
Anishinabek Nation
Governance Agreement
(2022), 50–51, 76, 102;
Gwich'in Comprehensive
Land Claim Agreement (1992),
65; James Bay and Northern
Quebec Agreement (1975),
25–26, 76; Maa-nulth First
Nations Final Agreement
(2011), 58–59; Nisga'a Final
Agreement (2000), 21, 26–27,
39; shíshálh Nation, 38–39;
Sioux Valley Dakota Nation
Governance Agreement
and Tripartite Governance
Agreement (2014), 76; Ta'an
Kwach'än Council Self-
Government Agreement
(2002), 59; Tla'amin Final
Agreement (2014), 102;
Tłı̨chǫ Land Claims and
Self-Government Agreement
(2005), 70, 86; Tsawwassen
First Nation Final Agreement
(2009), 81; Westbank First
Nation Self-Government
Agreement (2005), 27–28,
39, 51, 76, 102

self-reliance, 1, 33, 106, 130, 141. *See also* economic development
Semá:th First Nation, 10
Seminole Tribe, 114–16
settlements, negotiated, 14–15
shíshálh Nation, 38–39
Sioux Valley Dakota Nation Governance Agreement and Tripartite Governance Agreement (2014), 76
smallpox, 9–10
socio-economic issues, 91–97; death/injury of children and youth, 94; education, 36, 72, 86, 88, 92–93, 95–96; employment, 93, 111, 114; health, 36, 72, 91; housing, 46, 72, 93, 95; incarceration, 93–94; income and income tax, 79–80, 81, 93, 108, 114; self-government and, 94–97; suicide, 94
Songhees Nation, 138
sovereignty, 41–42
Squamish Nation, 70
Statement of the Government of Canada on Indian Policy (White Paper, 1969), 12–13
Status Indians, 1, 20, 62, 79–80, 107, 133. *See also* Indigenous Peoples
Stevens, Henry Herbert, vii, 17
Stó:lo First Nation, 10
Storyteller-in-Residence programs, Indigenous, 136
stumpage fees, 109
suicide, 94
Supreme Court of Canada, 14, 22, 23, 80, 121

Ta'an Kwach'an Council Self-Government Agreement (2002), 59
taxation, 79–81, 108–9
territory: overlapping, 125–26; Traditional, 54. *See also* land
Title. *See* Indigenous (Aboriginal) Title
Tla'amin Final Agreement (2014), 102
Tłı̨chǫ Community Services Agency (TCSA), 86
Tłı̨chǫ Land Claims and Self-Government Agreement (2005), 70, 86
tourism, 137
Traditional Territory, 54. *See also* land
Trans Mountain Pipeline expansion project, 123–24
transparency: financial, 67–70; leadership, 17–18
treaties: comparison to self-government agreements, 38–39; historic treaties, 35–37; modern treaties (comprehensive land claims), 35, 37–38
Treaty 8, 38
treaty commission process, 125–26
trustee-wardship relationship, 13, 14–15, 18, 43–44
Truth and Reconciliation Commission, Calls to Action, 88, 112–13, 135
Tsawwassen First Nation, 47–48, 109
Tsawwassen First Nation Final Agreement (2009), 81
Tsimshian, 21
two-generation rule, 20

unemployment, 93. *See also* employment
United Nations, 103
United Nations Declaration on the Rights of Indigenous Peoples: about, 31–33; Canada and, 32; on citizenship, 63–64; on economic security, 105; on Free, Prior, and Informed Consent, 117; full text of, 151–67; *Indian Act* and, 33; on languages, 83–84; on self-determination, 2. *See also* Indigenous Rights
United Nations Declaration on the Rights of Indigenous Peoples Act, 32, 117–18
United States of America, 32

Vale Canada Ltd., 110–11
Victoria: Reconciliation Contribution Fund, 138
Voisey's Bay Mine (Labrador), 110–11

water advisories, drinking, 102–3
Westbank First Nation, 47–48, 109
Westbank First Nation Self-Government Agreement (2005), 27–28, 39, 51, 76, 102
Wet'suwet'en First Nation, 54–55, 120–21, 122, 131
White Paper (*Statement of the Government of Canada on Indian Policy*, 1969), 12–13
Williams, Julie, 128
women, 62–63, 140
World Health Organization, 91
W̱SÁNEĆ Leadership Council Society, 136

Xwsepsum Nation, 138

Yesno, Riley, 130
youth and children, 94
Yukon: First Nation School Board (FNSB), 86, 96; Yukon First Nation Education Directorate (YFNED), 95–96

About Indigenous Corporate Training Inc.

INDIGENOUS CORPORATE TRAINING INC. (ICT) came to life in 2002 as a global training company. Founders Bob Joseph and Cindy Joseph have remained steadfast in their mission to create an Indigenous company to guide, train, and support learners in Working Effectively with Indigenous Peoples®. ICT is dedicated to fostering understanding, respect, and collaboration between individuals, organizations, and Indigenous communities.

Through ICT's training programs, resources, and partnerships, we aim to promote cultural competence, reconciliation, and the empowerment of Indigenous Peoples. The goal is to create positive and meaningful relationships that contribute to the preservation of Indigenous cultures and the advancement of Indigenous Rights, and to help to change the world for the better for everyone. Our training options are posted on **ictinc.ca**. To arrange for private training, please contact us at **ictinc.ca/contact-a-training-advisor**. If you would like additional information or opportunities to learn and share ideas with others, subscribe to our free Indigenous Relations Newsletter, available at **ictinc.ca/newsletter-sign-up** or scan this QR code:

photo: NATHAN SMITH

About the Author

~~~~~~

BOB JOSEPH, Co-Founder and President of Indigenous Corporate Training Inc. (ICT), has provided training on Indigenous relations since 1994. He has assisted thousands of individuals and organizations in building Indigenous relations. ICT's clients include all levels of government; Fortune 500 companies; financial institutions, including the World Bank; small and medium-sized corporate enterprises; and Indigenous Peoples. Bob has worked internationally for clients in the United States, Guatemala, Peru, and New Caledonia in the South Pacific. In 2006, Bob co-facilitated a worldwide Indigenous Peoples round table in Switzerland, which included participants from the United Nations; Australia; New Zealand; North, Central, and South America; Africa; and the Philippines.

Bob has worked as an associate professor at Royal Roads University and has routinely been a guest lecturer at other academic institutions. He has an educational background in business administration and international trade and is a certified Master Trainer, who, in May 2001, was profiled in an annual feature called "Training: the New Guard 2001" by the Association for Talent Development (formerly, the American Society for Training & Development). Bob was one of nine trainers selected for the feature from over 70,000 members who come from more than 100 countries and 15,000 organizations.

He is the developer of a multi-layer suite of training courses, including the following:

- Indigenous Awareness
- Indigenous Awareness: United States
- Indigenous Relations
- Indigenous Relations for Local Governments
- Indigenous Relations: United States
- *Working Effectively with Indigenous Peoples*®
- *Working Effectively with Indigenous Peoples*® *for Local Governments*
- *Working Effectively with Indigenous Peoples*®: *United States*
- Indigenous Consultation and Engagement
- Indigenous Employment: Recruitment and Retention
- Indigenous Procurement
- How to Negotiate with Indigenous Peoples
- Indigenous Relations Academy

Bob is also the author of books and resources about working with Indigenous Peoples, including *21 Things You May Not Know About the Indian Act*, *Indigenous Relations*, and *Working Effectively with Indigenous Peoples*® (the latter two co-authored with Cynthia F. Joseph).

Bob is an Indigenous person, or more specifically a Status Indian. He is an initiated member of the Hamatsa Society and has inherited a chief's seat in the Gayaxala (Thunderbird) clan, the first clan of the Gwawa'enuxw, one of the 18 tribes that make up the Kwakwaka'wakw. Bob is anticipating holding his inaugural Potlatch to confirm his chieftainship in the near future. His chief name is K'axwsumala'galis, which, loosely translated, means "whale who emerges itself from the water and presents itself to the world."